VIENNA

MARTIN HÜRLIMANN

VIENNA

A STUDIO BOOK

THE VIKING PRESS · NEW YORK

ENGLISH EDITION COPYRIGHT © 1970 BY THAMES AND HUDSON LTD LONDON
ALL RIGHTS RESERVED

PUBLISHED IN 1970 BY THE VIKING PRESS, INC.
625 MADISON AVENUE, NEW YORK, N.Y. 10022

SBN 670 74601 0

LIBRARY OF CONGRESS CATALOG CARD NUMBER: 70-87326

TRANSLATED FROM THE GERMAN 'WIEN BIOGRAPHIE EINER STADT' BY D. J. S. THOMSON

TEXT PRINTED IN ENGLAND BY COX AND WYMAN LTD FAKENHAM
MONOCHROME PHOTOGRAVURE PLATES PRINTED IN FRANCE BY ETS BRAUN ET CIE MULHOUSE

COLOUR PLATES PRINTED IN SWITZERLAND BY IMAGO ZURICH
BOUND IN ENGLAND BY COX AND WYMAN LTD FAKENHAM

CONTENTS

Aller heyligñ
en Sand Stef
Turn vnd an=
kait. Abgunn

Thuemkirch=
fan Mit dem
der schigklig=
deruebt. ??.

St Stephen's Cathedral: a Viennese woodcut by the Master A. F. in the Book of
the Saints of 1502

Some personal reminiscences

Wherever you go in Vienna, you will find memorial tablets surrounded by tiny red and white pennons and bearing the legend 'Eine Stadt stellt sich vor' (A City presents itself), constant reminders that this city is immensely rich in memories. I would like to adopt that same legend as the motto of this book. But who has the right to speak for this city? Which of the countless views of it should be photographed and selected? Which particular gems should be chosen from the vast storehouse of literary treasures? However much one may strive to be objective, to be impartial, this is, in the final analysis, a highly personal matter – and in Vienna even more so than elsewhere.

The 'real' Vienna . . . well, which is the real Vienna? Look at the long and yet by no means complete list of guide books on the arts, at the history of the Habsburgs which is still being written, at the literature with such names as Abraham a Sancta Clara, Grillparzer, Raimund, Hofmannsthal, Schnitzler and many more, at the great musical classics, at the Congress of Vienna, or at operetta after operetta, woven round the figure of old Franz Joseph with his side-whiskers and turned into films. For the modern taste: Otto Wagner, Gustav Mahler, Arnold Schönberg, Karl Kraus, Sigmund Freud, Schiele and Kokoschka. Or Adolf Loos, Anton von Webern, Ludwig Josef Johann Wittgenstein, to say nothing of the contemporaries. For the Americans: the Lipizzaner stallions at the winter riding-school, a tour in a horse-drawn cab or a seat at the Opera duly engineered by the hotel porter. A coach trip at night along the Kärntnerstrasse, blazing with light like a minor Broadway, out to Grinzing, where the young wine and the music combine to produce the traditional Viennese atmosphere. And, as backcloth to these colourful highspots, row upon row of houses from the late nineteenth and the twentieth centuries, built by men who showed more industry than artistic taste, no better and no worse than their counter-parts in Paris, London, Milan or Berlin.

And now a Swiss is offering to conduct you round. But before we set out on our tour of the past and the present, let me provide some evidence of my subjectivity by to some extent anticipating the final chapter on the most recent events and describing how I myself learned to love Vienna (not entirely uncritically).

1917

Prologue in Zurich. The 'imperial and royal' Hofburg Theatre company presented Grillparzer's 'Medea' in the Municipal Theatre; Hedwig Bleibtreu was in the great tradition of Burgtheater tragediennes; but at the same time she was already familiar with the world of Ibsen. Works by three contemporary dramatists were also performed: Schnitzler, Schoenherr and Salten, with Tressler in the famous conversational style which Heinrich Laube had introduced and which had become the hall-mark of the Burgtheater. A few months later: a complete season by the 'Theater an der Wien'. Lehár, Fall, Nedbal and Oscar Strauss conducted their own works; there was a positive orgy of waltzes and comic opera with a strong admixture of sentimental operetta, all spiced with the familiar Viennese dialect. Then, as the climax to the series of concerts by orchestras organized by the belligerent countries as a form of cultural propaganda, came the Vienna Philharmonic with Weingartner: the 'Symphonie fantastique' and the 'Eroica', the world-famous strings, the full-bodied horns, and withal the discipline of a great artistic ensemble and the unmistakable Viennese grace.

1919

The appeal by the famous children's doctor, Clemens von Pirquet, for help from America, where he had once practised, to deal with undernourishment and tuberculosis amongst Viennese children also found a response in Switzerland. My elder sister formed a relief committee and I was allowed to go with her to Vienna to hand over our contribution. Over the Arlberg in an unheated train – it was a long journey. But it took weeks for our wagon-load of gifts to arrive, so we had plenty of time to see Vienna. The old Emperor had died at Schönbrunn only three years before; the centuries-old Habsburg monarchy which he had bequeathed to his successor Karl was in process of liquidation. Vienna was at a loss. Had the realm which the imperial city represented been demolished at Saint Germain or had it gambled the empire away itself? Perhaps even tossed it aside wantonly? This city with its two million people was too big for the small German-Austrian State. The street lighting was cut and food rationed. The long rows of houses had a stale, spent look about them. Old ladies, determined to bear their poverty with dignity, went to great pains to serve a proper 'Jause' (coffee and cakes). But despite this undercurrent of sadness everyone spoke as if they were performing in some operetta, all Gabriels and Adeles, Idas and Olgas.

8

I View across the roofs of the inner town towards St Stephen's Cathedral with its lofty spire. The cupola in the left foreground belongs to St Peter's Church

I ST. PETER, ST. STEPHAN

And there still in all its splendour was the Royal Opera House – or had it already become the State Opera? Richard Strauss had only recently moved into Mahler's room as co-director with Franz Schalk. There was a repeat performance of the original production of 'Die Frau ohne Schatten': Maria Jeritza played the Empress, Karl Aagard Oestvig the Emperor, Lotte Lehmann the dyer's wife, Richard Mayr her husband Barak, Lucie Weidt the nurse, décor was by Alfred Roller and the conductor was Franz Schalk. A 'resident ensemble' such as I was never to witness again. Several times a week Strauss conducted; it was no 'gala' performance but simply the incomparable music-making of a master: 'Così fan tutte', 'Fidelio', 'Freischütz'. The most attentive, most critical and most appreciative audience was in the promenade, which was always packed. In Vienna everyone knew whether that night Jeritza was singing Tosca, and every change of cast at the Opera was discussed in countless parlours and drawing-rooms. The whole city lived music.

Then one evening a visit to Pirquet: noble features coupled with a noble spirit; an air of melancholy seemed to pervade the rooms of that elegant house – melancholy for the fate of Austria or the premonition of a more personal tragedy? Forty-eight years later I found myself quite unexpectedly standing before the grave in the cemetery where this, the finest of men, had lain since 1929.

1924

There was whipped cream again in Vienna. On his sixtieth birthday Richard Strauss, whose position as Director was being threatened by the customary local intrigue, gave the first performance of the ballet 'Schlagobers' (whipped cream) – a dancing Viennese café, which was invaded with almost revolutionary gusto by suburban 'Gugelhupfe' (Viennese cakes). The stirring waltz somehow just failed to move the audience but there was a charming Dance of the Tea Blossom as well as several other dainty morsels, and the Munich Strauss was as always good value. Although I was there as a music critic, I was in the mood to enjoy rather than criticize these special birthday performances at the opera and in the concert hall. The contest of the baton gladiators had not yet started; this was much more of a family occasion.

1933

Prince Eugene, that noble knight, had a great exhibition staged in his honour. In the Upper Belvedere *objets d'art* and souvenirs of all kinds were displayed, amongst them a gilded four-poster bed hung with tinkling 'putti', which had been specially made for the Prince's visit to a monastery. In the state-rooms of the Imperial Library, which housed Eugene's own unique library, one became aware of the passionate interest the great general took in what was going on in the realm of the arts. Here one was conscious only of an historic past, of a great soldier who won so many battles and who said: 'The desolation of war has its limits, and the laws of humanity should never be ignored.'

In the course of my work I met two men who had done much to preserve for posterity the historical traditions of Austria: Heinrich von Srbik, the historian, and Bruno Grimschitz, who had just finished his book on Lucas von Hildebrandt.

Why this special tribute to a great European, whom no one, with the best will in the world, could hope to present as a hero of German nationalism (a role that was imposed, willy-nilly, upon Maria Theresa), this truly imperial Field-Marshal whose victories were celebrated in an Austria torn between clericalism and Marxism and caught up in yet another upsurge of feeling in favour of Austro-German union?

1942

It had finally happened. The dream of a Greater Germany had suddenly been realized. Vienna was no longer a capital; Austria had become the Ostmark, part of the Third Reich. And one had not had to wait long for the inevitable war; final victory was once again a certainty. Although the Coventry-type bombing raids on German towns were growing in scope and intensity, to people on the Danube they still seemed comfortably remote, but the spirit had gone out of Vienna.

In my capacity as publisher, I met Rudolf Kassner and Richard Strauss. Both were hoping for better or at least different times. Kassner, who was unwell, was in bed when I called, but he had not lost his healthy sense of humour. We discussed the advances made in the science of physiognomy since Lavater, the relationship between the ear and the eye, and how, by a remarkable stroke of luck, Ferdinand Waldmüller had been commissioned to paint a portrait of the greatest of his Viennese contemporaries. And Kassner expressed his admiration of the artist's skill in 'making visible in and through the eyes the inner vision of Beethoven after his deafness'.

And in the Villa in the Jaquingasse, presented to him by the people of Vienna, the creator of 'Der Rosenkavalier', for once not in frock-coat on the conductor's podium but wearing a comfortable house-jacket, and, contrary to legend, completely relaxed and friendly – yet throughout that intimate conversation I was always conscious

12

of that imposing, almost frightening head, from which the score of 'Elektra' (which I once actually held in my hand) emerged flawless and complete. We discussed various possible publications. The old gentleman was particularly anxious that any personal correspondence that might be used in a biography should be scrutinized by my friend Willi Schuh in Zurich and should not be allowed to fall into the hands of the Third Reich's cultural propagandists. He took me into the unheated salon and showed me the famous Salome painting by an early Spanish master, but Frau Pauline's dishevelled head suddenly appeared in the doorway, scolding: 'I thought I told you not to go into this cold room!'

1947

Frontier-control by a Russian soldier. The Schwarzenberg Square was called – for the time being at least – Stalin Square. Perched on a tall pillar stood the bronze statue of a Soviet soldier carrying his banner. War wounds everywhere, not so terrible, perhaps, as in the 'Old Reich' but painful enough. The spire of the Cathedral was undamaged but the roof of the nave was a mere shell. The Opera House had been badly hit, particularly the stage – fortunately the foyer with its Schwind frescoes had escaped almost intact. The State Opera ensemble was playing in the Theater an der Wien, the Burgtheater in the Ronacher. The Albertina was half in ruins; on the square in front of it the Mozart Memorial had disappeared from its plinth – to be re-created later in the Burggarten.

This was all rather sad. But perhaps the whole thing was just another of those famous misunderstandings? This was not the first turning-point in world history and, despite the appalling hardships of the initial occupation period, people were somehow more composed than in 1919. Böhm was conducting and the Philharmonic was playing as superbly as ever. Maria Cebotari in the role of Salome kept alive the great tradition of Viennese operatic stars, though perhaps less prima-donnish, a little more human than her predecessors.

1955

In the Upper Belvedere, where the conqueror of Belgrade, surrounded by the generals of the Holy Roman Empire, had once received the ambassador of the Turkish Sultan, the Austrian State Treaty was signed and the Allied occupation forces withdrew. St Stephen's Cathedral and the Burgtheater had been restored and the Opera House was reopened in all its new splendour. The enormous stage was crowded with resident artists, the famous singers in the front row. Into the presidential box stepped the erect figure of the aged general and Social Democrat, Federal President Körner, with all the dignity of an emperor. The ceremonial opening in the morning was followed in the evening by a special performance of 'Fidelio', the everlasting song of freedom, a hundred and fifty years after that famous performance at the Kärntnertor before the crowned heads assembled for the Congress of Vienna. Crowds of people had gathered along the Ring and even the taxi-driver had his radio tuned in. The stalls and boxes inside the Opera House were gradually filling up with the modern, mid-century princes: motor-car tycoons and bank directors, filmstars and producers, Ministers and Press magnates. It was almost too much to expect any production, however super-lative, to compete with such a display of worldly wealth and distinction.

Afterwards I met Oskar Kokoschka with his wife Olda and Elizabeth Furtwängler in a 'Beisl'. How we missed Wilhelm Furtwängler, who had conducted the Vienna Philharmonic so superbly and who had kept the flame of Beethoven's genius alive in an age of death and destruction.

The restored Burgtheater also had its ceremonial reopening. Of the special perfor-mances I saw 'Don Carlos', and in yet another memorable performance by two great actors Schiller's lines cut through the charged atmosphere of the Burgtheater: father and son, king and prince; Philip, the ageing, gout-ridden monarch, bowed down by the burdens of office, plagued by his own, all too-human passions, and played by Werner Krauss with a subdued intensity that was almost uncanny; Carlos, whom Oskar Werner with all the impetuosity of youth presented as a dangerous rival.

1958

At the Künstlerhaus on the Karlsplatz there was a Kokoschka exhibition: the works of a seventy-two-year-old. He had been a member of the Viennese group formed by Josef Hoffmann, had moved in the same circle as Adolf Loos, Karl Kraus and Peter Altenberg, had become one of the founders of the expressionist drama in 1908 with his 'Mörder, Hoffnung der Frauen', had fought in the First World War as a volunteer in the Austro-Hungarian Army but spent the Second World War in London, branded by the Third Reich as a 'degenerate' artist. Could the questing spirit that was so much in evidence in that exhibition, a spirit that far transcended national prejudice, have sprung from any other place than Vienna with its exciting admixture of Slav blood?

Between the landscape visions and the mythical compositions inspired by Jerusalem and Thermopylae there were portraits of contemporaries, with the artist returning time and again to Vienna: Karl Kraus, Adolf Loos, Anton von Webern, Arnold Schönberg, Max Reinhardt, Princess Mechthilde Lichnowsky, Albert Ehrenstein, Alma Mahler. Then came the Raimund scenic designs for the Raimund plays and for 'The Magic Flute' . . .

1959

An international congress in Vienna: publishers from all over the world were meeting.

Austria also had its economic miracle – or was it perhaps a political miracle? It came somewhat later and was less spectacular than in Germany. The crises of successive wars and all that lay between them seemed to be things of the past; prosperity was more universal than ever before. Foreign visitors came pouring in again: Vienna was waiting for them; Vienna, a world metropolis in a small State, needed them. In the Schönbrunn palace, brilliantly floodlit, Federal Chancellor Raab received each Congress delegate with a handshake, before they all made for the buffets and some found time to admire the rococo splendour of the state-rooms. In the neo-Gothic rooms of the City Hall, where Lueger once held sway, stood the towering figure of the Mayor, Herr Jonas, welcoming the guests. Everything had been shared out peaceably between the two old rivals, the Austrian 'Volkspartei' and the Social Democrats.

The climax of the festivities was Mozart at the Opera House: with Karajan himself conducting, the 'Figaro' overture was soon casting its spell on the assembled book-publishers; Elizabeth Schwarzkopf, Irmgard Seefried and Christa Ludwig added their own special charm to the divine magic of the melodies, Erich Kunz's nimble bass seemed to dance round the majestic baritone of Eberhard Wächter's Count, and Günther Rennert directed with the hand of a master.

Outside the Währingerstrasse, not far from where Beethoven last lived, we visited Heimito von Doderer, author of the 'Strudlhofstiege'. He was to write for my publishing house the introduction to a book on Austria. A remarkable man, with one foot still in the old monarchy, the other in the atomic age! The walls of his bachelor apartment were hung with daggers, bows and arrows. Doderer was a very keen toxopholite. And, while we sipped whisky, he entertained us with his favourite subject, the dragons which, he assured us solemnly, still existed.

The Republic was still there and, it seemed, more secure than ever. *Ce n'est que le provisoire qui dure*. Without any of the wild enthusiasm of 1938, matter-of-fact but substantial, it had already lasted longer than number one. More foreign languages could be heard than ever before. Groups from the former vassal-states could be seen climbing out of motor-coaches. Was Vienna perhaps still the great capital of the Danube basin? Or would it take the first opportunity to lean once again on the strong right arm of the big brother? Had it perhaps found itself a new role as the meeting-point of the two super-powers, a sort of rest-house between East and West?

Here was I back in Vienna again with my camera: to put together a book on Vienna. Could I find a link between this astonishing corridor of history and the world of today? The world of today: it kept crowding in on me wherever I turned, at every church door and palace façade it was there demanding to be photographed, from the courtyards of the Imperial Palace to the meanest alley, everywhere it appeared in its bright steel and chromium suit made up in Wolfsburg, Turin, Oxford, Detroit or heaven knows where. Multi-storey buildings reared up; no sooner was a café or an old inn demolished than an expresso bar, an American bar, a grill-room or a Chinese restaurant had taken its place. Firms of all kinds were looking after the city's public relations, presenting the right image, while tourist agencies kept visitors on the move. There were also the social amenities: housing estates, kindergartens, open-air swimming pools, new parks, subways with escalators, some of which actually moved – the whole shooting-match. Why not Paris or London or Berlin? Why not Caracas, Rotterdam or Hong Kong? Well, why not? That is the question this book will try to answer.

The medieval city

Vienna lies, as everyone knows, on the beautiful blue Danube. But if you ask a foreigner who has just visited Vienna if he saw the Danube, the chances are that he will be unable to answer, and I have yet to meet anyone who found it blue. Very few visitors, having crossed the Danube canal into Leopoldstadt and moved on to the Prater, ever reach the great Danube bridges and the Left Bank, where the modern city with its new outlying suburbs stretches out to the fringe of the Lower Austrian plain, the scene of many a bloody battle between Germans, Bohemians, Hungarians and French. And here on the vast site of the 1964 Gardening Exhibition stands the Danube Tower with a rotating restaurant from which one has a panoramic view of the city. Protected on its north-eastern flank by the river, it lies in a semicircle on the fringe of the Vienna Woods: frontier-post of the Roman Empire, imperial capital on the border of the German states, heart of a Danubian empire that links – and possibly reconciles – the Germanic West with the Slav East.

The land on which Vienna stands today has been populated from time immemorial: archaeological remains date back as far as the Stone Age. The Illyrians, who settled here during the early Iron Age had already achieved a certain degree of civilization when the Celts introduced the La Tène culture around 400 BC. In the reign of Augustus the Roman legions reached the Danube and set up a camp in the 1st century not far from the frontier fort at Carnuntum; around AD 100 this camp was moved to where the Hoher Markt is today and was called Vindobona. The earliest recorded garrison was a cavalry regiment from Britain. The soldiers were followed by civilian population but before long the Marcomanni and the Quadi had broken through the Danube 'lines' and destroyed the young town. Under Marcus Aurelius it was rebuilt and tradition has it that the imperial philosopher died here during his Danubian campaign.

All historical traces of Vindobona were lost in the mass migration. In 433 the Danube province of Pannonia was occupied by the Huns. Then came the Rugli, Heruli and Langobards (whose sixth-century graves have been found), Slavs and Avars. Right up to the tenth century the place was only mentioned three times: Jordanis in his History of the Goths speaks of 'Vindomina' in the period around 450, the Salzburg Annals record a clash with the Hungarians at 'Wenia' in 881, and finally the Niederailach Year-books report that in 1030 the Germans were defeated by the Hungarians at 'Wiennis'.

In 976 the Emperor Otto II conferred the Margraviate of Austria (Ostmark) on a Franconian family, the Babenbergs; around 1135 Vienna also became part of the Babenberg domain and in 1137 was described for the first time as 'civitas'. But it was only after the Emperor Frederick I, Barbarossa, had raised the County to the status of a Duchy in 1156 that the first Duke, Henry II 'Jasomirgott' (1156–77) actually moved the Babenberg residence into Vienna. Duke Frederick II became involved in a dispute with the imperial authorities and in 1237 his adversary of the same name, the great Hohenstaufen Emperor Frederick II, rode into Vienna and made it an imperial city.

Vadianus. From Viennese woodcu of 151

Duke Frederick II was the last of the Babenbergs. He was followed during the interregnum from 1246 to 1276 by the Margrave of Baden and then in 1251 by King Přemysl Ottokar II of Bohemia. After a crucial battle on 26 August 1278 the victorious German king, Rudolf I, Count of Habsburg, entered the city and for the next six-and-a-half centuries the fortunes of Vienna were inextricably linked with those of the Habsburgs and their Austrian dynasty.

King Rudolf had also declared Vienna an imperial city, in order to protect it against encroachment by the King of Bohemia, but until recent times it has had to stand up for its rights. As late as 1897 the Emperor obstinately refused to recognize Dr Lueger's election as mayor. Several centuries earlier, three mayors who had fallen foul of the ruler were executed.

Vienna was the capital of the Duchy which in 1453 was promoted to Archduchy but not of all the Habsburg domains. Only some centuries later did it become the official residence of the Emperor and gradually it assumed the role of the largest and finest city in the Holy Roman Empire. In 1804 when the Habsburg Emperor Franz II assumed the title of hereditary Emperor of Austria, Vienna became the 'capital' of an empire.

'The Holy Roman Empire of the German Nation', which was always a slightly unreal institution, took its name from a city beyond its own frontiers. Rome symbolized a Western world united by Caesar and Peter, but it was not the seat of a central authority and in the Middle Ages there was no other imperial residence in which the power over all the various states and towns was concentrated. Earlier

II Console whi formerly support the foot of t organ in Stephen's Cathedr carved in his ov likeness by t cathedral's archite Anton Pilgra

18

RGELFUSS ST. STEPHAN: ANTON PILGRAM

Woodcut in the Schedel Chronicle of 1493

emperors moved from palatinate to palatinate and long after Paris had become the first city of France and London of England, Germany still had no capital. City republics such as Nuremberg and Regensburg, Cologne and Bremen were well established as commercial and cultural centres, when the German princes, fascinated by the methodical development of the French *état* and inspired by the absolutism of their day, were striving to turn their state residences into major capitals. This was the period when Vienna came into its own as the seat of the powerful dynasty which, from the close of the Middle Ages, was to assume the imperial crown almost automatically. And as the crown became more and more of a fiction, the men who wore it felt increasingly impelled to strengthen the power of the dynasty and of its centre, Vienna.

Vienna's role as Austrian capital has not always been clear and the complicated history of the Habsburg domains is also not made any clearer by the fact that, to begin with, succession was not by primogeniture. So on several occasions two or more brothers were ruling as joint or even as independent Dukes over Upper and Lower Austria, Carinthia, Carniola, Styria and Tyrol, and were also promoting the rival claims of such provincial capitals as Graz, Innsbruck and Linz, not to mention the Bohemian estates which emerged into the limelight from time to time. Of the Austrian Dukes on the imperial throne Maximilian I preferred Innsbruck, while Rudolf II, whose sole ambition was to destroy the Protestants, chose Prague rather than Vienna.

Among the historical monuments the visitor is likely to come across in Vienna the Middle Ages are not too well represented but they do have one architectural and one spiritual monument of outstanding importance: the Cathedral of St Stephen and the University.

In the twelfth century the Bishop of Passau, to whose diocese Vienna belonged, consecrated the eastern part of the Church of St Stephen. The remainder, including the Riesentor (Giant Portal), was added between 1230 and 1263, still in the romanesque style, but the ambition of successive Dukes to have a cathedral with its own resident Bishop was to remain unfulfilled for some time to come. The last of the Babenbergs, Frederick, assumed the right of patronage himself and appointed his Chancellor vicar. Under King Albrecht I, the first Habsburg to take up residence in Vienna, work was started on the Gothic choir (1304–40). Duke Rudolf IV laid the foundation stone of a new Gothic nave in 1359 and in 1364/65 he raised the status of the church to that of a diocesan foundation. In 1439 the great south tower, Vienna's symbol and most distinctive landmark, was completed but it was not until 1469 – in fact papal confirmation only came in 1479 – that the church became a diocesan cathedral. In the centuries that followed there were further alterations and improvements and finally, in the baroque period under the Emperor Charles VI, it became the official seat of the Archbishop. To what extent this building, which was not merely at the heart but was itself the heart of Vienna, owed its existence to the devotion of the citizens or to the generosity of their rulers is a moot point – in any case both played their part in giving not merely the Cathedral of St Stephen but also the entire old city of Vienna its very special character.

If the great cathedral was the hallmark of Vienna's religious pre-eminence, the University established it as a cultural and scientific centre. In 1348 the Emperor Charles IV had founded the University of the four nations – Bohemia, Poland, Bavaria and Saxony – in Prague, modelled on the university in Paris. In 1365 Austria's Duke Rudolf IV followed his example by expanding the school established by Duke Frederick II and making it the first German university. The number of Latin and Philosophy classes was increased and new courses in Medicine and Jurisprudence were added. In 1384 the Papal *placet* was given for the creation of a theological faculty. The University of Vienna became an important centre of humanistic education, one of whose most distinguished products was Joachim von Watt or Vadianus, whom Maximilian I crowned *poeta laureatus* and who subsequently became Burgo-

Tomb of Emperor Frederick III in St Stephen's Cathedral. Woodcut by Hans Burgkmair for the 'Weisskunig' the Emperor Maximilian I

23

Proſpect Der Reſidenz-Stadt Wien

DONAV CANAL

Vienna in the eighteenth century. Contemporary engraving

master and Reformer of St Gallen. Having gained a Master's degree in 1508, he became Rector in 1516. His Swiss compatriot Ulrich Zwingli had preceded him as a student at Vienna. By the time Maximilian I died in 1519, 'the city and the university of Vienna had', according to Conradin Bonorand, 'gained a key position not only in religious but also in political and cultural affairs'.

With his 'Reformatio nova', Ferdinand I gave the University a new constitution; it became more and more a State institution; the number of Protestants, who were particularly strongly represented in the medical faculty, was greatly reduced, and in 1623 Ferdinand II introduced a strict Jesuit régime. But under Maria Theresa, ably supported by her son, the spirit of enlightenment continued to flourish until finally, despite a series of reactionary setbacks, reforms were introduced in 1849–51 which guaranteed freedom of instruction.

The earliest University seal

The Saviour of Austria

The Habsburg Empire was still in the process of consolidation, with Vienna as its focal point, when it was subjected to its most severe test. A new power emerged in the east, advanced through the Balkans towards central Europe, sweeping everything before it, and even threatened the Holy Roman Empire itself. The Turkish Sultan Suleiman the Great, had conquered Belgrade in 1521, Pesth and Ofen in 1526, and his powerful army, ravaging and looting, was approaching Vienna. On 21 September the Turkish vanguard reached the outskirts of the city, which had been burnt to the ground by the inhabitants themselves in order to strengthen the main defences. On 26 September the Sultan himself arrived before the gates; Vienna was completely surrounded.

Suleiman boasted that within three days he would be dining in the Hofburg and, when his arrogant demand for surrender remained unanswered, he gave the order to attack. The Turks together with a motley collection of auxiliaries dug deep trenches right up to the city walls, which they planned to undermine and breach. The Archduke Ferdinand of Austria, brother of the Emperor Charles V, was in Prague and had entrusted the defence of Vienna to the royal Captain-General, Count Niklaus Salm, and to Philip, Count of the Rhine Palatinate and Duke of Bavaria. For two weeks attack after attack was launched against the walls and particularly fierce engagements took place around the Kärntnertor (Carinthian Gate). But when the third major assault had been beaten off, the Sultan suddenly decided, in view of the unfavourable weather conditions, the approach of winter and the news that a relief force under Charles and Ferdinand was on its way, to raise the siege, and on 15 October a solemn High Mass was held to celebrate the liberation of the city.

The second siege of Vienna by the Turks was no less dramatic. In 1683 a vast, motley Turkish force again appeared before the city walls, led by the Grand Vizier, Kara Mustapha. The Emperor Leopold I had left the city. The imperial army, which had to withstand the threat from the east, was commanded by Duke Charles of Lorraine, whose grandson, Franz, subsequently became emperor, but the Empire was also threatened from the west by the Most Christian monarch in Versailles, who had allied himself with the infidel. The defence of Vienna was entrusted to Count Rüdiger Starhemberg. Since the previous siege the fortifications had been greatly strengthened, but the Turkish attack was so unexpected that Starhemberg had his hands full, to begin with, preventing a general panic. Citizens and students were given emergency instruction in the use of weapons, while others were set to work strengthening the defences. Duke Charles and his cavalry were in the suburb of Leopoldstadt but they were much too weak to engage the enemy on their own. The other suburbs were once again destroyed by the defenders.

The siege began on 13 July and as the weeks passed the hardships of the defenders increased. There had been little change in tactics since Suleiman's time: while both sides exchanged artillery fire, the Turks again built their network of trenches and laid their mines, some of which at least the defenders were able to render harmless, and when the Janissaries and other élite troops of the Grand Vizier's army were not flinging themselves against the walls, the defenders were making desperate sorties. Starhemberg was wounded several times and, when he too fell victim to a dysentery epidemic, continued to carry out his duties from a litter. Duke Charles retired to the left bank of the Danube, where he awaited the arrival of the relief force. Eventually several princes rallied to the imperial army and joined up with a strong Polish contingent under King John Sobienski. On 12 September a decisive battle was fought at Kahlenberg, where the Turks were defeated, and on 14 September the Emperor re-entered Vienna.

One of the younger recruits to the imperial army was a twenty-year-old whose elder brother had already fought against the Turks and had fallen in an earlier battle. This young man, fresh from his studies in Paris, acquitted himself with remarkable bravery and the Emperor promised him command of the first regiment that became free. So began the long and distinguished career in the service of Austria and of the German Empire of a man whose name was to appear under many highly important state documents, a name that in itself betrayed his trilingual origins: Eugenio von Savoy.

Vienna had been liberated but it was the subsequent victories and the statesmanship of Prince Eugene, who became known as the Saviour of Austria, that liberated the Empire from the twofold threat of Ottoman and French power-politics and thereby paved the way for Vienna to blossom out as a brilliant imperial capital.

Seen in retrospect, the fame achieved by Eugene seems strangely unorthodox. This outsider, who could not even speak German properly, does not fit into any national

III The *Schweizerto* (Swiss Gateway of the Hofburg built 1552 at th instigation of th Emperc Ferdinand

history curriculum, and the dialectical historian is completely at sea with this 'Roi des honnêtes hommes'. On the other hand, this finest of soldiers was worshipped by his men and became the pet general of peace-loving poets. Hugo von Hofmannsthal and Ricarda Huch waxed lyrical in his praises. Anyone who tries to see Vienna merely as a 'German' city will have to overlook Eugenio von Savoy, but the real imperial city, the most truly European in the whole of Europe, had no more fitting or more brilliant exponent than the noble occupant of the town palace in the Himmelpfortgasse and of the Belvedere.

Eugene came from a branch of the House of Savoy. His father's grandmother was a daughter of Philip II of Spain, so the Emperor Charles V was one of his forebears. His Italian mother was a niece of Cardinal Mazarin. He grew up at the court of Louis XIV at Versailles and the King had marked him out for holy orders. The 'Roi Soleil' always addressed the puny, unattractive boy, who was dressed in a soutane, as the *petit abbé*, but the pious Liselotte, Duchess of Orleans, noticed with marked disapproval that Eugene kept company with a group of young noblemen who engaged in immoral pleasures. In this charmed circle Eugene also frequently appeared in female clothes. As the King denied him the military training he longed for, the young man, fired by the example of his late brother, made a secret get-away with his friend, the young Prince Conti, son of the Great Condé. The King, who was furious, had them pursued but their pursuers only caught up with them at Frankfurt, beyond the frontiers of France. Prince Conti was persuaded to return but Eugene preferred to continue alone. He sought out a cousin, the Margrave of Baden, in the imperial army, and under his command was allowed to fight his first battle.

After receiving his baptism of fire at Kahlenberg, the Prince threw himself into his new profession with tremendous enthusiasm. He was a Major-General at twenty-two. While storming Buda, his horse was shot from under him and he was wounded twice. When he was thirty, he received his Marshal's baton from the Emperor, who also placed him in supreme command of the operations against the Turks.

That great Austrian, Hugo von Hofmannsthal, gave his own, self-critical assessment of what Eugene meant to Austria: 'A world of enemies before him; but what a world behind him: sprung from a root, the root-evil of Austria, but thrusting upwards in a thousand young shoots; always the same root: spiritual lethargy, mental apathy, the slight twinge of a sense of duty, the instinct to escape from unpleasantness into some kind of diversion, though not, as a rule, into wickedness but a much worse, more hateful type of evil, a heavy, stifling materialism – struggling against all this to the very end and never tiring, conqueror and creator, who worked with unresponsive material – a man, a great and good man and concealed in him the mystery of all mysteries: creative nature.'

Eugene's achievements were richly rewarded by the Emperor. He showed admirable discretion in administering the fortune which he rapidly accumulated from the favours bestowed on him. As soon as he was in a position to do so, he paid off his youthful debts and he took an active interest in the financial affairs of the monasteries of Casanova and San Michele, while they were under his supervision, and he retained the title of Abbot to the end of his days. As Head of the Privy Council and President of the Imperial War Council his political status was second only to that of the Emperor; from 1715 to 1725 he was Governor-General of the Netherlands, although he never actually lived there, and the Imperial Assembly in Regensburg elected him Imperial Field-Marshal.

Even during his campaigns Eugene continued to take an active interest in his palaces and his collections, which did so much to enhance Vienna's cultural reputation. In 1694/95 he had bought several houses in the Himmelpfortgasse and commissioned the court architect, Johann Bernhard Fischer von Erlach, to build a town palace. But before the work had been completed, he changed architects and entrusted the remainder of the work to Lucas Hildebrandt, a pupil of Borromini who had built his fortifications during the campaigns in Piedmont in 1695/96, and who designed a summer residence on a site which he had acquired in 1693 outside the city walls. Dominique Gérard, a pupil of the great Lenôtre, planned the landscape terracing and Hildebrandt built the Lower Belvedere, which was followed a few years later by the even more splendid Upper Belvedere with its spacious state-rooms – an architectural masterpiece which aroused the admiration of contemporaries far beyond the borders of Austria.

The palace in the Himmelpfortgasse was extended in 1708, when the adjacent house was demolished, and the interior was again magnificently designed and decorated; the Prince took a lively personal interest in the work of the architect Claude le Fort du Plessy, the stucco-worker Bussi, the sculptors Giovanni Giuliani and painters Chiarimi and Louis Dorigny.

Eugene's collections were as unusual as the collector himself. They included astronomical instruments, historical portraits, a collection of paintings and an

Prince Eugene of Savoy. Engraving by C. Weigel

32

Two scenes from the Siege of Vienna by the Turks in 1683

exquisite cabinet of engravings. Three rooms of the palace were given over to the splendid library. A menagerie contained both tame and wild animals, and in the gardens of the Belvedere were rare plants from all parts of the world. All of which testified to the catholic interests and exquisite taste of the *grand seigneur*, who amidst this splendour led a simple bachelor life in his simple snuff-stained smoking-jacket.

34

Engravings by R. de Hooghe, Amsterdam

In 1712, when Eugene was in London on a political mission, he spent his spare time browsing around bookshops. He was in the habit of looking through every book that was sent to him and, if his interest was aroused, of reading it before he handed it over to his bookbinder. In this way he became familiar with contemporary works appearing in French, amongst them *La Théodicée* by Leibnitz, whom he also came to know personally while the philosopher was in Vienna from 1712 to 1726. At considerable cost he engaged Etienne Boget, son of Louis XIV's bookbinder, from Paris and, when this highly cultured Frenchman eventually became his librarian and cultural secretary, another master-binder, Martin Tourneville of Brussels, was engaged to produce the elegant morocco-bound volumes with the arms of Savoy; after Eugene's death, Tourneville became attached to the court. Georg Wilhelm von Hohendorff, a Prussian who was for many years the Prince's Adjutant-General, was also his political confidant and acted as his agent in the purchase of books and old manuscripts; Hohendorff himself left a very fine library of six thousand leather-bound volumes, which, like Eugene's own library, passed into the possession of the Emperor Charles VI and, as the Bibliotheca Hohendorffiana, forms a valuable part of the present State Library. In his choice of engravings the Prince relied mainly on the judgement of a leading connoisseur, Pierre-Jean Mariette. From Prince Elbeuf he received three of the first statues found at Pompeii. The enchanting bronze statue of the boy praying, from the Lysippos school of the fourth century BC, came from the collection in the Château de Vaux-le-Vicomte and after Eugene's death it found its way to Sans Souci, having been acquired by King Frederick II of Prussia, who as Crown Prince had spent some time at the ageing Field-Marshal's headquarters and took after him in so many ways. The remaining collection of pictures and sculptures was divided up except for a number of paintings which went to form the nucleus of the Turin Gallery.

The first impression Prince Eugene made on the visitor was one of coolness and reserve, but this soon disappeared in conversation as he warmed to his subject. Although his features have been described as 'not at all pleasant', there was a look in the eyes that held others in thrall. Lady Montague reported that 'he passes for a free-thinker'. Among his visitors was Montesquieu, the famous author of the *Lettres Persanes*. An indication of Prince Eugene's fame throughout Europe is the fact that the Abbé de Saint-Pierre sent him his *Projet de Paix Perpetuelle* to which Kant later lent his support, and the Prince expressed his approval. The group of friends whom he occasionally joined in the evening to play taroc included a Bohemian, Wenzel Wratislaw, the Portuguese Ambassador Tarouca, a Dane named Berkentin, an Englishman, Lord Waldgrave, the Imperial Vice-Chancellor, Count Schönborn, and the Papal Nuncio, Domenico Passionei, who later became a Cardinal and who shared the Prince's dislike of the Jesuits and of any form of fanatical intolerance. Eugene's relations with the poet Jean Baptiste Rousseau remind one of Frederick the Great's subsequent friendship with Voltaire, except that Eugene reacted to the malicious tirades from the French side with more calm and dignity than did the King of Prussia.

Eugene was not altogether averse to female company, particularly in his later years. He was a not infrequent visitor at the soirées of the sparkling Dorothea, Countess of Rabutin, was a friend of Countess Maria Anna Althan, known as 'Spanish Althan', and a favourite source of Viennese gossip was his relationship with Countess Batthyány, the raven-haired 'beautiful Lori', who had been a widow since 1703. It was said that the Isabella greys in their pink harness had become so accustomed to drawing the state carriage of Savoy from the Himmelpfortgasse to the Palais Batthyány that they could find their own way and would wait patiently at the doorway while their aged master, his ancient coachman and his equally ancient lackey went on sleeping. A familiar figure about town was also Signor Accriboni, 'the old Prince's beautiful wardrobe-master'; he arranged Eugene's brilliant receptions, was also much sought after in other palaces to organize balls and finally organized at his own risk masked balls in the great hall of the Mehlgrube, entry to which cost one ducat but was reserved for the cream of society.

Despite his lively interest in international affairs, Prince Eugene's loyalty to the Emperor never wavered and he showed no interest in the Czar's offer of the crown of Poland. He seldom took part in official State functions. Foreign ambassadors were in the habit of calling on him when they arrived or left but it was only at the receptions given for the special envoy of the Sublime Porte that a large number of people gathered at the Himmelpfortgasse to feast their eyes on such rare displays of Oriental pageantry; on these occasions the Prince himself appeared in his richly frescoed state-room in the full splendour of his unique position, surrounded by all the imperial generals, wearing the Order of the Golden Fleece, the diamond-studded dagger of honour lying on the table before him.

Eugene, who had grown perceptibly weaker with advancing years, died on 21 April 1736 in his palace in the Himmelpfortgasse. The final tribute was paid by the Emperor who commissioned Lucas von Hildebrandt to design a magnificent catafalque in St Stephen's Cathedral, such as would normally have been reserved for the monarch himself.

From Baroque to Rococo

Throughout the period when Vienna was in process of becoming an imperial capital and a cultural centre, relatively few of the city's medieval monuments were preserved, but the original layout of the old city round St Stephen's Cathedral remained intact. Hardly a house survived from the period before the first Turkish siege. The mode of living of the nobility in the seventeenth and eighteenth centuries, the emergence of a prosperous middle class and the drive of the entrepreneurs and the collectives in the twentieth century all left their mark, and yet the narrow alleyways have almost all survived, huddled together in the great network of fortifications, the bastions of which had to make way last century for the Ring. Around the city the outlying villages with their princely estates and their vineyards continued to prosper, forming an inner circle within the Line Wall, while beyond that spread the new workers' tenements and factories of the industrial era.

An English visitor in 1668, Dr Edward Browne, was impressed by the size and the cosmopolitan character of the city even before the second Turkish siege. A hundred years later Diderot and d'Alembert, writing in the *Encyclopédie*, were less impressed by the buildings that had gone up since then. They remarked upon the dirty alleyways, but not even the Gothic sculpture on St Stephen's Cathedral appealed to their enlightened minds: 'Entirely surrounded by walls, bastions and ditches, Vienna has none of the elegance of those cities in which avenues with an abundance of gardens, summer-houses and other ornamental features provide a special charm . . . Vienna has none of those wide streets which lend beauty to a city; the only possible exception is the New Market square, thanks to the new or restored buildings surrounding it. The main church is in the Gothic style, decorated inside and outside with arabesque ornaments in stone. The new Jesuit church, on the other hand, is beautiful in design.'

During the same period the London Doctor of Music, Charles Burney, who visited Vienna's musicians in 1772, gave the following description of the city: 'The streets of Vienna are rendered doubly dark and dirty by their narrowness and by the extreme height of the houses; but as these are chiefly of white stone and in a uniform, elegant style of architecture, in which the Italian taste prevails, as well as in music, there is

IV The southern façade of the Upper Belvedere seen through the south gate of the Belvedere. The coat of arms of the House of Savoy surmounts the stonework on either side of the gates

38

something grand and majestic in their appearance, which is very striking; and even many of those houses, which have shops on the ground floor, seem palaces above. Indeed the whole town, and its suburbs, appear, at first glance, to be composed of palaces, rather than of common habitations . . .'

In the *Encyclopédie* the suburbs were given special mention: 'The outlying suburbs present a more imposing appearance than the city itself, because they were entirely rebuilt after the last siege by the Turks.' Lady Mary Wortley Montague in her frequently amusing description of her journey to Constantinople in 1717 was also delighted by these suburbs: '. . . I never saw a place so perfectly delightful as the Fauxbourgs of Vienna. It is very large and almost wholly composed of delicious palaces; and if the Emperor found it proper to permit the gates of the town to be laid open, that the Fauxbourgs might be joined to it, he would have one of the largest and best built cities in Europe. . . .'

The glorious Baroque period opened with the arrival of the Jesuits from Rome and it was Italian builders, sculptors, stucco-workers and painters who, to begin with, dominated church architecture almost entirely or at least set the tone.

The former Carmelite church 'am Hof' was given a baroque room by the Jesuits in 1607–10 and in 1662 the splendid façade was added. In 1631 – again under Jesuit supervision – work began on the University church of Maria Himmelfahrt and in 1709/10 Andrea Pozzo carried out the interior decoration. In 1622–74 Cipriano Biasino and Antonio Carnevale together with Jakob Spatz built the new Dominican church.

There is such an abundance of bas-reliefs and burnished gold altars, such an endless vista of domes, of painted architecture and of cunningly-placed windows, that the visitor who enters by way of one of these majestic façades has an overpowering sense of the theatrical. The thunder of the organ with its ornate screens and soaring pipes, accompanied by the melody of the violins and the clamour of the drums and trumpets, mingles with the jubilant voices of the angel-choirs.

This artistic extravagance was not confined to the churches; it spilled over into secular architecture and reached its climax in opera. In 1652 the Emperor Leopold I, who was an ardent patron of music and the theatre, summoned the theatre architect Giovanni Burnacini from Mantua and his son Lodovico Ottavio eventually became the chief Court Engineer and spent twenty-five years in the imperial service. During this period he designed the scenery for no less than a hundred and fifteen operas. His

visual imagination, uninhibited by tradition, found no satisfaction in creating a static décor which would stand the test of time. Burnacini's designs and the engravings of his décors with their ingenious transformation devices give one some idea of the tireless imagination of this greatest of all scenic artists. But if the visitor to Vienna does not find time to explore the National Library with its priceless collection of theatrical treasures, he can at least see a specimen of Burnacini's design-work in the Column of the Holy Trinity on the Graben, which Leopold I erected as a token of thanksgiving for the ending of the plague.

Other outstanding scenic artists were Ferdinando Galli-Bibiena from Bologna, who was first employed by the future Emperor Charles VI in Barcelona, and his sons Guiseppe and Antonio. With a magnificent sense of perspective, they managed to conjure up palaces with enormous state-rooms, temples and vast gardens, apparently endless caverns and Elysian Fields. The 'grande e magnifico teatro', which Francesco Galli-Bibiena, Ferdinando's brother, built for Ferdinand in the Burg in 1706 unfortunately disappeared, as did the theatre built by Burnacini on the Cortina in 1665.

No less emphemeral than the theatrical décors were the triumphal arches erected for imperial weddings or for the entry of a newly-crowned ruler, and the catafalques (castrum doloris) set up in the churches to commemorate the exalted dead: such work brought the architect just as much honour as the building of a palace.

Of all the buildings which provided a permanent setting for the social life of the Habsburg court and of the princely and autocratic families that attended it, the imperial residence naturally took pride of place. And yet it never achieved completion as one coherent whole, although the Emperor had at his disposal not merely a host of Italian artists with their superior traditional skills but also three native architects – two of whom have already been mentioned in connection with Prince Eugene's palaces – who were among the greatest of their time: above all Johann Bernhard Fischer von Erlach, whose son Joseph Emmanuel worked with him and eventually succeeded him, and their self-willed rival, Johann Lucas Hildebrandt.

Born in 1656, Johann Bernhard Fischer, whose father was a sculptor in Graz, was profoundly influenced by his period of apprenticeship in Rome under the aged Bernini. On his return to Austria he gave the future emperor, Joseph I, who was then King of Hungary, lessons in architecture. In 1696 he was ennobled and adopted the title 'von Erlakhen' from his mother's family, and in 1705 he was appointed 'Superintendent of all Imperial Court and Pleasure Buildings'. There is an aloof grandeur

The Town Palace of Prince Eugene in the Himmelpfortgasse showing 'the arrival of the Aga dispatched by the Gran

ceived in audience on 9th April of the year 1711'. From the *Entwurf einer Historischen Architektur* by Fischer von Erlach about his palace façades and interiors which makes his work, including the palaces he built for the nobility, seem like a synthesis of Roman baroque and the French classical style. This sense of far-reaching affiliations within the entire context of the 'orbis terrarum' is also reflected in his own splendid engravings for a universal history of architecture, the first of its kind.

Fischer had assisted with work on the Plague Column in the Graben, designed by Burnacini. Apart from Prince Eugene's town palace, his outstanding works in Vienna were the Batthyány-Schönborn Palace, the Bohemian Court Chancellery and the Trautson Palace. He built the impressive doorway of the Lobkowitz Palace. The climax of his career came when he designed the Court Library in the Burg and built the church in honour of St Charles Borromeo, patron saint of Charles VI. Both works were unfinished when he died and were completed by his son.

Joseph Emanuel Fischer von Erlach was almost as versatile as his father. His studies, subsidized by the court, had taken him to various countries; he had visited Paris and the Low Countries, as well as England, where he took a special interest in mechanical engineering, which enabled him on his return home to build a steam-driven pumping-machine for the Schwarzenberg Garden and a much admired 'fire-machine'. He struck up a friendship with Leibniz when the latter came to Vienna, collected works of art and built up a valuable library.

The Palais Trautson. From the *Entwurf einer Historischen Architektur unterschiedener berühmter Gebäude* by Johann Bernhard Fischer von Erlach, Leipzig 1725

While the splendid designs of the elder Fischer von Erlach give only a vague impression of that proud master of the Baroque, the personality of his great rival, Johann Lucas Hildebrandt – known to his contemporaries as Gian Luca – who in 1730 was also ennobled, is comparatively well documented. Although his copious correspondence with Prince Eugene has not survived, the letters Field-Marshal Count Harrach wrote to his brother give a detailed account of the difficulties these noble patrons encountered in dealing with their architect.

Among Hildebrandt's many activities was the creation of a technical device for regulating the flow of the river Wien in 1713 and the construction of several triumphal arches and catafalques. Besides various palaces and his masterpiece, the Belvedere, he was also responsible for two churches which, together with St Charles's, rank as the most important late baroque churches in Vienna: St Peter's and the Church of the Piarists. With his volatile temperament and his love of baroque splendour, he defended his plans with a passion which obviously did not make for smooth relations even with such a well-disposed patron as Prince Eugene. On one occasion Count Harrach groaned: 'The accursed Jean Luca is a regular beast for magnificence. When I wish to suppress something or to economise, Jean Luca howls like a man possessed. It can't be done, it can't be done, my honour and reputation are at stake.'

The Hofburg in Vienna seems to the modern visitor little more than a row of buildings and courtyards, planned and built over centuries, beginning with the 'Schweizertrakt' of Rudolf of Habsburg and finishing in the nineteenth century. The single grand design was never fulfilled, not least because the imperial budget was chronically overspent.

Entry into the medieval part, which was rebuilt several times, is through the Swiss Gate, designed by the Renaissance master, Pietro Ferrabosco. The 'Stallburg', previously known as the Ebersdorf Palace, was built in 1558–65 as the residence of the Archduke, later Emperor Maximilian II, and in 1575–88 the 'Neue Burg', the present Amalienhof, was built for Rudolf II. In 1660–68 the master-builders Carlo Martino and Domenico Carlone were commissioned by Leopold I to link up the three existing buildings on the basis of plans by Philiberto Lucchese, and the result was the 'Leopoldinische Trakt', which, after a fire in 1668, was restored by Carlone to a design by Pietro Tencala.

Johann Fischer von Erlach, then the Emperor's chief architect, had barely started to build the Imperial Library when he died in 1723. In the same year his successor,

Hildebrandt, began work on the north wing of the Imperial Chancellery, but after only two years his post as Superintendent of Imperial Buildings was given to Joseph Emanuel Fischer, who continued the work on the Imperial Library and the Chancellery, but his masterpiece was the Winter Riding School, one of the most elegant late baroque buildings in Vienna. In 1767–83 Nikolaus Pacassi built the side wing to the library building, thus completing the magnificent group surrounding Joseph II Square, in the middle of which an equestrian statue of the Emperor has stood since 1807.

In the nineteenth century yet another tremendous effort was made to complete the imperial residence but the time was past when the ruler himself was the life and soul of court festivities and a patron of all the arts; the Emperor was leading the modest life of an ordinary bourgeois citizen, he was quite satisfied with the simple camp-bed of the professional soldier and preferred an hour strolling in the park and chatting with Katharina Schratt, actress at the Imperial Theatre, to the pomp of the court. But it had become essential for the monarch to keep up appearances, to nurture the patriotism of the new electorate that was now emerging.

While every leading noble family had its summer and winter palace, suburban 'garden villas' became increasingly popular with members of the royal household, particularly after the threat of an enemy siege had finally been removed and the nature-loving eighteenth century had dawned.

The imperial Favorita – also known as the New Favorita to distinguish it from the Old Favorita of the Augarten – dates back to the early seventeenth century. Destroyed during the Turkish siege of 1683, it was rebuilt by Ludovico Burnacini and with its island theatre was the scene of many festive occasions, especially under Leopold I. It was here that Maria Theresa spent her youth but, following the death of her father, Charles VI, in the palace, she ceased to use it; in 1746 she sold it to the Jesuits and since then it has undergone a number of structural alterations, has been encroached upon more and more by the growing city, and has been used as an educational centre.

Under Maria Theresa, Schönbrunn became the favourite summer residence of the court. Leopold I instructed his court architect, Johann Fischer von Erlach, to build a residence suitable for the heir to the throne on the site of his modest hunting-lodge. Fischer drew up a grandiose design: the gentle slope of the hillside was to be crowned by a far more elaborate building than the present one, something more like the Belvedere that Hildebrandt subsequently built, although that too is less pretentious. But the Emperor's funds were limited, so the over-all proportions were reduced and

V Ceiling painting
with trompe-l'œi
architecture by
Gaetano Fant
is a feature o
the staircase of the
Palais Kinsky
formerly th
Palais Dau

The Inner Court of the Hofburg with the Imperial Chancellery, 1780–90

the main building was situated at the lower end of the park. Fischer's building was altered several times, particularly by Maria Theresa who had a storey added by Nikolaus Pacassi and the interior redecorated in the rococo style of her own time; she also had the gardens, originally laid out by Jean Trehet, redesigned by Jean Nicolas Jadot. Whereas Italian baroque was the predominant style in the seventeenth century, it was gradually replaced in the eighteenth by the more elegant, courtly culture of France, especially in interior decoration, and more and more French landscape gardens as well as French architects and decorators came to Vienna. During this period a number of palaces belonging to the nobility were also reconstructed and decorated in the rococo style.

Ferdinand von Hohenberg added the final touches to Schönbrunn; he built the palace theatre and with the construction of the Gloriette in 1775 completed the layout of the gardens. The palace remained the favourite residence of the imperial family. Napoleon used it when he occupied Vienna in 1805 and 1809; his son, the Duke of Reichstadt, grew up here and recited Corneille and Racine in the theatre. And Francis Joseph lived throughout almost the whole of his long reign at Schönbrunn.

Viennese society on the threshold of social revolution

When Maria Theresa, Charles VI's eldest daughter, succeeded to the Habsburg throne at the age of twenty-three and became mistress of the Archduchy of Austria and the Kingdoms of Bohemia and Hungary, she appointed her husband, Duke Francis Stephen of Lorraine, and later also her son, Joseph II, co-regent, but she alone bore the burden of all the major decisions of domestic and foreign policy, even after her husband had been elected German Emperor as Francis I in 1745. Her forty-year reign was far from uneventful; her ability to rule was tested to the utmost. One has only to remember the Silesian War, in which she pitted her resources against the most formidable of opponents, Frederick II of Prussia. How she succeeded, despite her preoccupation with affairs of state, in remaining such a remarkably devoted wife and mother and providing her ten grown-up children with so much loving guidance is one of those personal mysteries, but the explanation must lie partly in the spirit of the age in which she lived and even in the character of Vienna itself.

Maria Theresa was a devout Catholic and she tried, by censorship and police supervision, to inculcate in her people the moral principles which she impressed upon her own family. But at the same time her strongly developed maternal instinct inclined her to tolerance and undoctrinaire pragmatism. In Prince Kaunitz she chose one of the most cultured men in Vienna to advise her, and her absolutism was not only enlightened but imbued with humanity.

Her eldest son, Joseph II, who became German Emperor on the death of his father in 1765, was of a very different temperament. Deeply influenced by the ideas of the Enlightenment, he kept urging his mother as co-regent to introduce reforms. After his first meeting with the young Emperor, Frederick the Great wrote to Voltaire: 'I have seen the Emperor, who is preparing himself to play a great part in Europe. He was born in a bigoted court and has thrown off superstition; he was brought up in pomp and has adopted simple habits; was nourished with incense and is modest; is devoured by a desire for fame and sacrifices his ambition to a childlike sense of duty, which he truly fulfils most conscientiously; has only had pedants for teachers and yet has enough taste to read Voltaire's works and appreciate their merit. He once recited to me almost an entire canto from the *Pastor fido* and several verses from Tasso.'

In the early part of Joseph's ten-year solo reign from 1780 to 1790 one reform after another was introduced: the abolition of serfdom, the dissolution of the religious orders and the distribution of their property, religious tolerance and relaxation of censorship, poor-relief and an improved health service. But as these reforms went hand in hand with an increase in central authority, public enthusiasm was accompanied by considerable secret opposition. In 1782 Pope Pius VI paid a personal visit to Vienna in an unsuccessful attempt to remind the Emperor of his duties as a Catholic; the Prince of the Church, who was also an impressive personality, was naturally received with full honours, was entertained for a month in the Imperial Palace with every mark of respect, and the populace flocked to the pontifical masses and blessings, but the Emperor gave not an inch of ground on his policy towards the Church. Like so many public benefactors, Joseph was by nature an autocrat, and posterity has not yet decided to what extent his high-minded, visionary spirit is to be admired or his lack of prudence and foresight to be condemned. In any case, 'Josephinism' struck deep roots in Vienna, and even a century of reactionary government failed to eradicate it from the minds of its citizens.

Joseph, who died childless, was succeeded by his brother, Leopold II, who, though perhaps not quite so enlightened, was certainly the more stable character. As Grand Duke of Tuscany, a title inherited from his father, he had carried through some notable administrative reforms; as Emperor, however, he was destined to rule over Germany and Austria for only two years, too short a time for him to make any appreciable progress towards the constitutional monarchy which was clearly his objective.

His son, Francis II, accepted the implications of the so-called Napoleonic New Order in Europe, and in 1806 he relinquished the title of Emperor of a German 'Holy Roman' Empire which had become a mere fiction. But two years before, as ruler of the hereditary Habsburg domains, he had assumed the title of Emperor of Austria and it is as Francis I of Austria that he has survived in history – as good Emperor Francis, so touchingly immortalized in Haydn's 'Kaiserslied', host to the Vienna Congress, who, through his brilliant and versatile Chancellor, Prince Metternich, did much to inaugurate a new era of Great Power politics. Metternich wielded the power until the revolution in 1848 and must be held mainly responsible for the completely reactionary régime which proved so much more tenacious than Joseph's noble ideals. One of his contemporary critics, the dramatist Grillparzer, who regarded the prince as a brilliant

Emperor Joseph I.

Emperor Charles VI in coronation robes

diplomatist but a bad statesman, paints a somewhat different picture from that of the traditional monarchist historians:

'The Emperor Francis, illiberal and narrow-minded, had decided to prevent any innovation in his State. Short-sighted and yet, within the limits of his vision, clear-sighted, he introduced for this purpose a degree of police oppression, which is almost without parallel in recent history . . . Prince Metternich, who was by nature a charming, cultured man but who in the early part of his career was inclined to be frivolous and was always governed by his appetite for life (in the better sense of the word), had become the foremost critic of the repressive measures introduced by his master, the Emperor Francis. He and his intimate associates ridiculed the pedantic outlook of the Austrian state authorities, and his enthusiasm for Lord Byron and similar liberal minds showed conclusively the extent to which any debasement of human nature was contrary to his own nature. But when the Emperor Francis died, he had grown old, complacent and arrogant. Ten years earlier he might perhaps have welcomed reforms and, as he was idolised by the government officials, might well have carried them through. But now he was only interested in remaining in the same old rut.'

Francis I's sickly, insignificant successor, Ferdinand 'the Kind', left the running of the State to the four-man 'State Council', which was dominated by Metternich and under which the Austrian ship-of-state drifted towards the hurricane of 1848.

When Charles de Montesquieu visited Vienna in May 1728, he was struck by the fact that the men at the top were highly accessible and that there was close contact between the Imperial Court and the ordinary citizen. 'The number of foreigners here is so large that one is both a foreigner and a citizen. Our language [French] is so widely spoken that it is almost the only one used by people of importance and Italian can almost be dispensed with. So many different nationalities are represented here that they must of necessity have a common language, and they will always choose our French.'

Statements of this kind indicate how much ground the native German had lost, although Vienna was to play an appreciable part in establishing its role in world literature and as the *lingua franca* of the Danube Basin.

The Viennese spirit of easy-going companionship, which transcended class-barriers and which proved stronger even than the cosmopolitanism of the capital, undoubtedly owed not a little to the proverbial charm of the Viennese women. The Turk Evliya Celebi, when he visited Vienna in 1665, was filled with admiration at the gallantry with which women were treated even by the highest in the land: 'Whenever the Emperor meets a woman in the street, if he is on horseback, he pulls up his horse and waits for the woman to pass. And if the Emperor is on foot and meets a female person, he remains standing politely. Then the woman greets the Emperor and he removes his hat and bows to the woman, and only when she has passed does the Emperor continue on his way.'

At the beginning of the nineteenth century the Prussian musician Reichardt in his 'Confidential Letters' described what delighted him most in Vienna's busy, colourful streets and public gardens: 'The whole morning until one o'clock the Augarten was filled with a happy, graceful throng like a wonderful show-garden, and never have I seen so much beautiful skin, so much tender, voluptuous flesh in such beautiful garments. And the clarity, friendliness and tenderness in the bright, brown eyes, the allurement of the full, red lips, the delicately rounded chin and the inexpressibly soft contour of the round cheeks. Nothing about these lovely creatures seemed artificial or contrived.'

There was a sober yet decorative background to the sociability of the Viennese, like a fixed horizon on the stage which seems to be constantly extended as the lighting changes, namely, the Catholic Church. As patron of the arts, the Church had already outpaced the secular power. From the passionate sermons of Ulrich Megerle, who adopted the evocative name of Abraham a Sancta Clara, at the time of the plague to the pomp and pageantry of high feast days, the Church offered the Viennese a spiritual home, in which they felt themselves well protected and pleasantly uplifted by the saintly host winging its way towards heaven. Inclined to tolerance rather than to intolerance, they were more attracted by the sort of childlike piety that is reflected in Joseph Haydn's music than by the glowing faith of the Jesuits.

In the sixteenth century Austria had come very close to turning Protestant. Under the more tolerant Archdukes the 'German sickness' had spread rapidly and had gained a militant following, especially among the nobility. If the Habsburgs had not clung obstinately to the traditional faith, the new doctrine would have triumphed. When Ferdinand I himself asked the Pope and Ignatius Loyola to send Jesuits to Austria, the Protestants were already well-established, especially in the University, and it was not until 1578 that the intolerant Rudolf II was bold enough to dismiss a non-Catholic who had been elected Rector. By the seventeenth century the entire education system was once again firmly in the hands of the Church. Nevertheless

Leopold I found it necessary to issue a decree in 1675 which forbade any more non-Catholic booksellers to settle in Vienna. But such regulations proved ineffective against the Viennese thirst for knowledge, and in 1736 the Archbishop Count von Kollonitsch complained that only three of Vienna's thirteen booksellers were Catholics; he also drew attention to the large number of Protestant merchants and manufacturers. Evangelical churches were forbidden, but the faithful could always congregate in the chapels of Protestant ambassadors. Finally in 1781 Joseph II's 'Edict of Toleration' created the sort of situation that was more in keeping with not merely the Viennese temperament but also the supra-national character of the imperial capital. And the present Archbishop was certainly speaking from the heart when he addressed the Second Vatican Council so persuasively in favour of the ecumenical movement.

Nothing in the social life of Vienna since the Middle Ages has left such painful memories as the treatment of the Jews. The grim chapter of Jewish persecution can never be erased from Vienna's history, any more than the fact that not all Jews were entirely without responsibility for the popular feeling against them. The public burning of two hundred and ten Jews in 1421 was one of the most horrifying single examples of barbaric persecution prior to Hitler's holocaust. Time and again the unfortunate Israelites were subjected to humiliating bans of all kinds and yet those in high places never seemed able to dispense with their financial skill. A Jewish Edict issued by Ferdinand I in 1551 required members of the Jewish community to wear a yellow ring sewn to the left breast (in Hitler's time it was the Star of David), and in the seventeenth century it was a favourite sport of students to flog Jews under the benevolent, lenient eye of a devout Rector. In 1669 Leopold I banished Jews once more from the city, but this did not prevent the merchant-firms of Wolf Schlesinger and Löw Sinzheim from continuing to do business under special licence. In 1677 Oppenheimer founded the house that bore his name and played an important part as 'imperial war-agent and Jew'. It was only with the Enlightenment that normal co-existence with the Israelites became feasible – in principle at least – but Lessing's *Nathan der Weise* could only be staged after long negotiations with the censorship, and even then in truncated form. Unfortunately the Jewish problem in Vienna was by no means over.

The history of the Viennese freemasons is not quite so grim. Maria Theresa had no patience with this new male fashion. Her husband, Francis Stephen, on the other hand, had already joined a Lodge in London and in 1742 was present in complete secrecy at the foundation of the Viennese Lodge. He was in the highly congenial company of representatives of noble families such as the Salms, Starhembergs, Trautmanndorffs, Windischgrätzes and Zinzendorfs. Maria Theresa, hearing that her ban had been ignored, had the meeting-place raided by the police on 7 March 1743, but her young husband was able to escape in time by way of an underground passage. Francis Stephen, who was shortly afterwards elected Emperor, did not allow even the Papal Bull against the Freemasons in 1751 to shake his loyalty to his brother-masons and when he died in 1765 he had become Grand Master, without apparently undermining his very happy marriage. But the game of hide-and-seek went on until Joseph II finally lifted the official ban on freemasonry and such a pious character as Mozart, to say nothing of his friend Haydn, felt no inhibitions about joining in the mysterious ritual of his Lodge. The strains of the 'Masonic Funeral Music' and 'The Magic Flute' give these sites a quite unworldly significance. But even the Freemasons were panic-stricken by the news of the revolution in Paris and they sent a deputation to the Emperor to inform him of their patriotic decision to dissolve their Lodge 'until times were more settled'. The gentlemen were graciously received and Francis II finally dismissed them with the dry remark: 'Perhaps we shall soon have more settled times again.'

For the time being, however, the situation even in Austria was far from settled. Napoleon's armies were rampaging through Europe and twice the proud imperial city had to accept the humiliation of a French occupation. In November 1805 and again in May 1809 the Corsican set up his headquarters in the Palace of Schönbrunn. On 15 August 1809 Napoleon's birthday was celebrated with great pomp; the citizens of Vienna were commanded to line the streets for the great march-past of the troops, the houses were hung with flags, all the church bells rang and many worthy Viennese, among them the young Grillparzer, found that their curiosity to see the Emperor was stronger than their anger.

In the midst of this turbulent period, towards the end of 1807, Madame de Staël made her appearance in the salons of Vienna and occasionally on Thursday evenings held literary court. She found the Viennese, who flocked to meet this interesting adversary of Napoleon, good-hearted and well-mannered but she missed the intellectual agility of the Parisians. Her friend and escort, August Wilhelm Schlegel, offered to give a series of lectures on dramatic art to private subscribers, but Emperor Francis,

VI The Church of St Charles, built 1716–39 to the designs of J. B. Fischer von Erlach. The spiral reliefs on the two columns depict scenes from the life of St Carlo Borromeo, after whom the church is named

who at that time would seem to have had little else to preoccupy him, declared: 'Schlegel is on no account to be given permission to hold lectures'; but finally he was persuaded to change his mind and the lectures were given under the watchful eye of a police commissar.

After Napoleon had presented himself to the Viennese as a conqueror, he insisted on becoming the son-in-law of their legitimate Emperor, and on 17 March 1810, as a prelude to the wedding ceremony in Paris, the bethrothal of the Empereur with the Archduchess Marie Louise took place in the Church of the Augustinians. Napoleon was not present in person but was represented by the same Archduke Charles who had defeated the greatest general of the day at Aspern.

Following the Corsican's abdication, Vienna was the obvious place in which to hold the most famous and most glittering of all Congresses. On 22 September 1814 the Kings of Württemberg and Denmark and the Grand Duke of Saxe-Weimar made their ceremonial entry, a few days later the Czar of Russia and the king of Prussia were conducted into the city by the Austrian Emperor with appropriate marks of honour, and they were followed by the King of Bavaria. Among the delegates who assembled on 2 November with Prince Metternich were the victor of Waterloo, the Duke of Wellington, the Prussian Chancellor, Hardenberg, and his ambassador in Vienna, Wilhelm von Humboldt, and representing France, which even without Napoleon was still a force to be reckoned with, was the brilliant Talleyrand. Many of the gentlemen had brought their ladies and until the Congress ended on 11 June 1815 there was a constant round of social functions: court balls and private balls, masquerades and tableaux vivants, merry-go-rounds and fireworks, outings by carriage or on horseback, sleigh parties and hunts.

Then Vienna resumed its normal, carefully censored day-to-day life and once again the passage of time seemed to have been arrested. But the placid good nature of the Viennese was not entirely immune from the world outside; the heyday of the coffee-house had come. During the Turkish sieges the Viennese had become coffee-conscious and had soon realized that the young wine of the Nussberg need fear no hot competition but that, on the contrary, the two were admirably complementary. The municipal authorities and the central administration vied with one another in issuing licences to coffee-refiners, and in the eighteenth century the Viennese coffee-house ceased to model itself on its older cousins in Paris and London and took on more and more a character of its own. Now in the new century, at the Café Bogner in the

Singerstrasse one could meet the musician Franz Schubert with his friends, the painter Schwind and the playwright Bauernfeld, while Herr Neumer's Silbernes Kaffeehaus was frequented by Grillparzer, Lenau, Anastasius Grün, Raimund and many others. The princely houses held musical soirées at which not only the latest work of a Viennese maestro was played but also the most recent composition from abroad, and in the literary and intellectual life of Vienna the salons of the Schwarzenbergs and Metternichs were rivalled only by the receptions given by the much-travelled Joseph Hammer-Purgstall or the rising dramatic star Karoline Pinchler. Regardless of the general ban on the formation of societies, larger circles grew up in all secrecy, and became the scene of lively discussions. One example was the 'Concordia', which included among its members Grillparzer, Bauernfeld, Prince Friedrich Schwarzenberg, the court actor La Roche, and the painters Waldmüller and Kriehuber, and which met at an inn called 'Zur Kaiserin von Österreich', where prominent foreign visitors such as Andersen, Berlioz, Félicien David and Liszt were also given an enthusiastic welcome.

Everyone complained of the censorship, which was apparent everywhere. The sins committed by the watchdogs of politics, morals and culture would fill volumes. The Viennese intelligentsia found such relief as it could in complaints and jokes but, for all the grousing that went on – and it is not entirely unknown in Vienna today – one is left with the uneasy suspicion that even under Metternich's rod of iron certain people managed to lead quite an agreeable life. And even among the censors themselves there were those who frequented the coffee-houses not just to spy but also to join in the whispering campaigns and have a look at foreign newspapers.

The most popular social meeting-place in Vienna was undoubtedly the theatre; only here could one expect to find a cross-section of all classes and make oneself felt. In music and drama Vienna had reached maturity at a time when politically it had barely reached the state of puberty. Connoisseurs of music flocked to Vienna from all over Europe and it was the ambition of every virtuoso and composer, singer and actor to make his name with this cosmopolitan audience. For that reason alone, although it is extremely difficult for the camera to do justice to music and drama, any verbal description of life in Vienna would be incomplete without them.

City of Music

The very name 'Vienna' has long had a special association with music. Other cities also have their cathedrals, their splendid palaces and all the intellectual and worldly attactions that any capital has to offer but unique to Vienna is this concentration on music, which within three generations, from Gluck to Schubert, produced in the 'Wiener Klassik' the richest harvest of Western music.

This was no chance phenomenon. Paris acquired its brilliance from the fact that it was the focal point of a great nation; Vienna had developed its own *genius loci* over centuries, which clearly cannot be recorded in this book, partly because much of it is no longer visible on the face of the city. Historical monuments had to make way for new buildings; the piano, which until recent times could be found in every private house, has been replaced by internationally manufactured mechanical devices, and even Vienna's concerts and operas have moved into the world orbit of the flying 'stars'. And yet in this wonderful city there is still more than enough to remind the visitor, wherever he goes, that he is surrounded by music: it was here that Mozart chatted with Joseph II, in this house that the Chevalier Gluck died, there is the great hall of the ancient University where old Haydn was acclaimed at a performance of 'The Creation', in this palace Beethoven held one of his famous Academies, and now you are standing before the house in which Schubert was born – symphonies, oratorios, quartets, operas without number winging their way out into the world.

Music: an art practised by emperor and people alike. The crowned heads set the example. Rudolf of Habsburg counted famous Minnesingers among his personal friends. Duke Rudolf IV, patron of the University, founded a new court orchestra. Maximilian I, although his main residence was in Innsbruck, reorganized the court orchestra in 1496–98, made Vienna its permanent base and gathered some of the outstanding musicians of the day around him: Paul Hofheimer was ennobled by him, Heinrich Isaak appointed court composer, and Ludwig Senfl, who had come to Vienna as a boy chorister in 1495, was summoned back in 1517. Ferdinand I also assembled a number of important musicians in order to revive the orchestra which had been disbanded on his father's death; he increased the number of singers and instrumentalists from thirty-seven to eighty-three. The Thirty Year's War interrupted the musical life of the court once again, but Ferdinand II was generous in his support of the orchestra. His successor, Ferdinand III, was himself no mean musician: he composed masses, motets, hymns, a Stabat Mater and a musical drama. During his reign the Dutch, whose influence had been paramount, were replaced by the Italians, who dominated the scene for almost the next two centuries. The same emperor was responsible for bringing to Vienna the Fugger Music Library, which is today one of the most priceless possessions of the National Library.

In the imperial family a full musical education was regarded as *de rigueur*. For Leopold I, an unprepossessing little man who was highly conscious of his exalted position and heard Mass three times a day, music was a sort of private profession. During his forty-eight-year rule four hundred new operas – almost entirely by Italians – and oratorios were performed and he frequently contributed one or more arias to the operas of his court conductor, Draghi.

Joseph I too was a cultivated musician. In 1708 he had the Opera House rebuilt and between twelve and fourteen new works were performed there each year. Charles VI was a pupil of Johann Josef Fux, the first Austrian to win for himself with his Italian operas a place of honour among the Ariostis, Bononcinis, Caldaras, Scarlattis and Zianis. In 1718 Charles engaged the famous Zeno as court poet and when the latter expressed a desire to return to Italy in 1729, the no less famous Metastasio. Apart from Fux, the native talent was represented by Georg Reutter, his son Johann Adam Georg and Georg Christoph Wagenseil.

Charles VI not only secured the Habsburg throne for his daughter Maria Theresa, he also schooled her admirably for the task of presiding over the dawn of the great classical period of music. Wagenseil was her teacher; she played the piano and competed in singing with the other young princes and princesses. She once remarked jokingly to the celebrated prima donna Faustina Hasse, wife of the composer, that she regarded herself as the 'first' virtuosa in Europe, as her father had insisted on her singing a song at the early age of five on the private stage in the palace. And indeed playing music and acting were the favourite pastimes at court. In 1772 Monsieur L'Augier told Dr Burney, who was on a visit from London, that the Empress, who since the death of her husband had given up all forms of amusement, had been an exceptionally good singer in her youth: 'In Florence she sang with Senesino [famous singer, 1680–1750] such an excellent duet that her very beautiful voice and her graceful, sophisticated demeanour moved old Senesino to tears.'

64

On 16 October 1762 Leopold Mozart sent his friend Hagenauer in Salzburg an account of the friendly reception he had been given at Schönbrunn. In 1761 Hasse had been invited to Vienna by the Empress, where this master of Italian-German opera lived until 1773. Christoph Willibald Gluck in the course of his wanderings felt more and more at home in Vienna, particularly since his marriage to a Viennese in 1750. And Joseph Haydn was impatient to return from Esterház to Vienna: the golden age had dawned.

The Emperor Joseph II seemed exceptionally well qualified to stimulate at the highest level the growing self-consciousness of German culture and help it to break free from Italian and French domination. In 1776 he decreed that the special theatre next to the Burg (or imperial palace), which was significantly called the 'théâtre français', should become the 'German Court and National Theatre' and should be exclusively devoted to German drama. Like his predecessors, Joseph had received a thorough musical education, had a bass voiced trained in the Italian school, played the viola and the 'cello but was particularly gifted as a pianist and accompanist. After the midday meal he was in the habit of practising for an hour, three times a week together with other instrumentalists. His personal taste was still influenced by the Italian tradition as represented by his court conductor Salieri, but he also had a great respect for Mozart's talent, appointed him to succeed Gluck as court composer in 1787, attended all the premières of his operas and also many of his concerts.

Leopold II, formerly Grand Duke of Tuscany, had little time during his two years as emperor, to concern himself with music. On the other hand, his second son Rudolf is well known to musical historians as the pupil and patron of Beethoven. The heir to the throne – the Franz of Haydn's 'Imperial Hymn' – was a keen music-lover and played the violin regularly in quartets, but under this stiff-necked gentleman music became a routine at court. Until 1824 Salieri remained court conductor; his successor was called Joseph Eybler – who any longer remembers his name? The long reign of the distinguished patrons was over, German music had become autonomous, the age of Enlightenment had given way to the age of Revolution, the age of Napoleon, the age of Beethoven.

'Indeed, Vienna is so rich in composers, and encloses within its walls such a number of musicians of superior merit, that it is but just to allow it to be, among German cities, the imperial seat of music, as well as of power.' Dr Burney, who wrote this in 1772, also gives an instance of the universal popularity of music. 'At night two of the poor scholars of this city sung, in the court of the inn where I lodged, duets in falset, soprano and contralto, very well in tune, and with feeling and taste. I sent to inquire whether they were taught music at the Jesuits' college and was answered in the affirmative . . . After this there was a band of these singers, who performed through the streets a kind of glees: this whole country is certainly very musical. I frequently heard the soldiers upon guard, and sentinels, as well as common people, sing in parts.'

Burney visited the 'admirable poet' Metastasio, whom he rated even higher than Racine; he saw Hasse, Wagenseil and Gassmann and gave a detailed account of his visit to the old Chevalier Gluck, 'one of the most extraordinary geniuses of this or perhaps of any age or nation . . . Gluck recounted to me the difficulties he had met with in disciplining the band, both of vocal and instrumental performers, at the rehearsals of Orfeo . . .' On 5 October 1762 the memorable première of this first 'Reformoper' had taken place in the Burgtheater, naturally in Italian, after Gluck had already become famous for his music to several of Metastasio's Italian dramas and Favart's French comedies.

In 1781 Mozart finally settled in Vienna and wrote to his sceptical father: 'I assure you that this is a Splendid place – and for my métier the best place in the world.' Somewhat later, when he had become better acquainted with the harsh reality (in other words with what would today irreverently be called intrigues), he wrote rather more pointedly: 'The Viennese are people who enjoy shooting – *but only in the theatre* – and my profession is too popular here for me not to be able to support myself. This is certainly the piano country.'

The maestro still had ten years of life before him and he wrote work after work for performances in Vienna and on tour. It is not even possible to say now when or where many of these, including, for example, the incomparable last three symphonies, were first performed. In 1782 'Il Seraglio' appeared, in 1786 'The Marriage of Figaro', the following year 'Don Giovanni', especially composed for Prague, in 1790 'Così fan tutte', and finally in 1791, the year of his death, 'The Magic Flute'.

Joseph Haydn had spent most of his life between 1761 and 1790 at Esterház. When Prince Nicolaus's orchestra was disbanded after his death, Haydn, already a famous maestro with an imposing range of compositions of every form, finally settled in Vienna. His friendship with Mozart, who was twenty-four years younger, bore fruit in the most mature string quartets of both the masters. Between them they virtually founded this particular genre of music, to which Beethoven also had recourse for expressing some of his profoundest thoughts; the noblest form of 'house music', it still brings professionals and amateurs together in many a Viennese home. Haydn and Mozart themselves played quartets to their friends and both particularly enjoyed playing the viola.

Haydn – we are referring naturally to the famous Joseph not to his brother Michael, who was also extremely gifted and who lived and worked in Salzburg – reached the climax of his career during his two visits to England in 1791/92 and 1794/95, which inspired his London symphonies. The public performances of the two great works of his later years, the oratorios 'The Creation' (1798) and 'The Seasons' (1801), were acclaimed by his own contemporaries as 'historic events'. For the lighthearted age, in which music was essentially of the period and for the period and in which premières were the order of the day, had given way to a much more exacting, much less limited age of 'humanity', and the man who was to give the fullest expression to this new sense of liberation was already living in Vienna.

Beethoven was twenty-two when he came to Vienna in 1792. He studied composition under Haydn, who was proud of his pupil but never achieved the same intimate relationship with him as with Mozart. Following Mozart's example, Beethoven gave piano recitals and was soon performing in the houses of the nobility, where his forceful personality and his self-assurance made an immediate impression. His playing lacked the perfection of Mozart but it had a dynamic brilliance of its own and showed wonderful depth of feeling in the slow passages.

Beethoven fought his battles like a Field-Marshal. And in Vienna he had at his command a public with an insatiable thirst for music. At the unlikely hour of seven o'clock on Thursday mornings music-lovers would gather in the Augarten, where both Mozart and Beethoven performed some of their compositions for the first time. And in the private palaces one concert followed another. At Prince Lobkowitz's, for example, where his private orchestra played the 'Eroica' from the original score months before it was performed in the houses of the bankers Würth and Fellner, to be finally given its official première in the Theater an der Wien, at that time the largest auditorium in Vienna. With the 'Eroica' – then called simply Symphony in E Flat – Beethoven broke all the known conventions, but his genius was in no danger of being misunderstood. His opera 'Fidelio' admittedly failed to make an impression in its first version but people were talking about this elegantly dressed composer

VII 8 Grinzinger-strasse, where Beethoven lived for a while at the same time as the writer Grillparzer's family

68

GRINZING: BEETHOVEN-GRILLPARZER-HAUS

with the brusque manner who was moving from salon to salon, consorting with counts and princes as if they were his equals, basking in the homage of titled women. Then he was assailed by deafness. A tragic figure, isolated by his own mistrust, he became irritable and unkempt. But his was no longer a private life; this was the age of Rousseau and Napoleon, in which the great man's afflictions were the affliction of his time and his destiny the destiny of a heroic exponent of freedom.

Beethoven is said to have changed his lodgings more than sixty times, but for the most part he lived in the outskirts of the city, frequently spending the summer in Baden. Once he lived in Heiligenstadt next door to the Grillparzer family.

No composer before him had so many visitors, Germans, French and English among them. Beethoven also met Goethe and other great men of his day. During the Congress of Vienna a special performance of 'Fidelio' – now in its third and final version – was given before an audience of emperors, kings and princes, and on the birthday of the Empress of Russia Beethoven took part in a concert in the Hofburg, at which Francis I presented him to the other monarchs.

The tremendous length of the programmes which musicians and audiences were accustomed to in Vienna at that time is shown by Beethoven's Academy on 22 December 1808 in the Theater an der Wien: it included not only the first performances of the Fifth and Sixth Symphonies but also two sections of the Mass in D, the Aria 'Ah perfido', the Piano Concerto in G Major with the composer as soloist, to say nothing of the customary impromptu performance on the piano by the impresario, and in conclusion a new Choral Fantasia. But how far short these performances were of accepted standards today can be seen from Reichardt's account of this memorable concert:

'Poor Beethoven, who at this concert had made the first and only net profit of the entire year, had met with considerable opposition and only feeble support in organizing and carrying through the performance. Singers and instrumentalists were composed of very heterogeneous parts, and it had not even been possible to arrange a complete rehearsal of all the pieces, which were full of the greatest difficulties . . . Every movement [of the Pastoral Symphony] was a very long, completely coherent passage full of vivid paintings and brilliant ideas and figures. And in consequence this Pastoral Symphony lasted longer than an entire court concert is expected to last . . . The eleventh piece was a long fantasia, in which Beethoven revealed all his mastery, and, in conclusion, another fantasia in which the orchestra and finally even

71

the choir joined. This singular idea came to grief in the performance through such complete confusion in the orchestra that Beethoven in his artistic zeal thought no more of the audience or the place and called on them to stop and begin all over again.'

An outstanding event was the first performance of the Seventh Symphony in the great hall of the University on 8 December 1813, the same hall in which Beethoven had attended a special concert in honour of Haydn. The sensation of the evening was undoubtedly a special composition entitled 'The Battle at Vittoria' with its fanfares and percussion, but what excited the music-lovers was the Allegretto in the Symphony, which had to be played at once *da capo*. The concert was repeated four days later – again with an enthusiastic demand for the *da capo* of the Allegretto – and early the following year Beethoven conducted the same works in the great Redoutensaal with the further addition of his latest symphony, the Eighth.

At the first performance of the Ninth Symphony with the choral finale based on Schiller's 'Ode to Joy', the Viennese were again fully conscious of witnessing an historic event. Admittedly the maestro Rossini had been given an equally jubilant reception two years before but that was no more relevant than the triumphs of Johann Strauss were to the honour paid to Brahms. The Viennese always had a welcome for the Muses, however light they might be, and even Beethoven did not think it beneath his dignity to help out a simple country orchestra or to write variations on a song he had heard in a suburban theatre. And the good-natured, humble yet splendidly frivolous creator of the 'Barbiere', while he was in Vienna, personally intervened in a legal action on behalf of the deaf composer.

Beethoven's last lodging was in the Schwarzspanierhaus (which has since disappeared), where Stephan von Breuning, his childhood friend from Bonn, was also living with his family. The little Gerhard von Breuning with his merry chatter passed the time for the lonely bachelor, plagued by dropsy, in his roomy, chaotically untidy lodging. One of his last visitors was young Ferdinand Hiller, who was brought to the maestro's sickbed by his teacher, Johann Nepomuk Hummel. 'A few days later,' he wrote in his memoirs, 'on 26 March 1827, while we were enjoying the happiest of company in the house of Herr von Liebenberg, the art patron, we were surprised by a violent thunderstorm between five and six. A heavy snowstorm was accompanied by loud thunderclaps and lightning-flashes that lit up the room. A few hours later guests came with the news that Ludwig von Beethoven was no more – he had died at a quarter to six.'

Never before had Vienna witnessed such a funeral as on the afternoon of 29 March 1827. The schools were closed and many thousands followed the coffin. Eight Kapellmeisters, including Weigl, Hummel, Seyfried, Kreutzer and Gyrowetz, were the pall-bearers. Among the torch-bearers were Schubert, Czerny and Grillparzer.

Among those who followed Beethoven to his last resting-place was Franz Schubert, the Viennese schoolteacher's son, who could not even afford a piano and who completed score after score – operas, symphonies, chamber music and, above all, songs and more songs – until he too, at the early age of thirty-two and only a year and a half after Beethoven, was carried to the Währing cemetery (both bodies were later transferred to special graves in the Central Cemetery).

Schubert never left his lower-middle-class environment; he never consorted with kings and emperors; the heroic age had passed. But the well-spring of music showed no sign of drying up; in Vienna people sang and played more than ever. His contemporaries, however, could scarcely be expected to appreciate the rich feast that Schubert – evoking the acme of bliss and plumbing the depths of melancholy with his inspired use of the major and the minor key – set before them. Ten years after Schubert's death, when Robert Schumann visited Vienna, where his wife Clara had already made her name as a pianist, he was still able to unearth one of the finest treasures: the great Symphony in C Major. And in March 1840 he wrote as follows:

'The musician who visits Vienna for the first time may be enchanted for a while by the splendid clamour of the streets and may have paused more than once in wonderment before the tower of St Stephen's, but he is soon reminded of a churchyard that lies not far from the city and which is more important to him than all the sights of the city, the last resting-place of two of the finest exponents of his art. And so, after those first few tumultuous days, many a young musician like myself must have found his way out to the Währing cemetery to place his tribute of flowers on those graves or merely to plant, as I did, a wild rose on Beethoven's grave. As I had not been privileged to meet these two artists, whom I revere most highly among the modern artists, while they were still alive, I would have wished to have at least someone by me who had been close to one of them and preferably, I thought, one of their brothers. It occurred to me on my way home that Schubert's brother Ferdinand, of whom, I knew, he had thought highly, was still alive. Before long I called on him. He knew me from the frequent tributes I had paid to his brother. He let me see the compositions by Franz Schubert in his possession and the sight of this pile of treasure sent a thrill of joy through me: where to begin and where to stop! Amongst others he showed me the scores of several symphonies, many of which had never even been heard and, in some cases, had been started only to be pushed aside as being too difficult and turgid. Who knows how long the symphony we all talk of today might have remained undiscovered and laden with dust, if I had not obtained Ferdinand Schubert's agreement to send it to Leipzig to the management of the Gewandhaus concerts or to the artist himself [Mendelssohn] who directs them . . .

'It is true: this Vienna with its St Stephen's tower, its beautiful women, its air of pageantry, girdled by the countless convolutions of the Danube and reaching out to the lush plain which rises gradually into the towering mountains beyond, this Vienna with all its memories of the greatest German masters must be fruitful ground for the musician's imagination . . . In a Schubert symphony, in the clear, rich, romantic vitality of it, I am reminded of Vienna more vividly today than ever and I realize again why this particular environment should have produced such works. . . .'

The Great Redoutensaal in the Hofburg during a masked ball.   Engraving by Josef Schütz

City of the Theatre

Inextricably linked with music in its dominance was the theatre. In his History of the Burgtheater, Rudolf Lothar made the somewhat oversimplified statement: 'The theatre has been cultivated in Austria, poetry never.' Vienna did not produce a Shakespeare or an impressive array of world-famous dramatists to compare with such musicians as Gluck, Haydn, Mozart, Beethoven and Schubert. Vienna was only one of many German theatrical centres, although perhaps the most exciting. Unlike Paris with its unbroken series of sensational premières, it was not the focal point through which everything a great nation had to offer was channelled to the outside world. Vienna cultivated its own local genius but it attracted an unusually high degree of cosmopolitan talent and absorbed all kinds of national traits from neighbouring countries, which contributed to that unique mixture of geniality and humour, that Viennese love of the theatre which has always been rooted in the character and the idiom of the people.

It took a long and historic process of gestation to give birth to a work like 'The Magic Flute', which was essentially a product of Vienna but at the same time became the property of all mankind: the sacred plays of the Middle Ages, the humanist comedies of Terence, the English comedians whose popular theatre achieved such triumphs in central Europe, the clowns and puppet-shows in the market-places, the pomp of the court festivals and finally the opera, which was hailed with enthusiasm immediately after its first appearance in Italy as the most complete, the ideal expression of the Baroque period – all this fell on fertile soil in Vienna, involving everyone from emperor to coachman.

When the Jesuits were summoned to Vienna around the middle of the sixteenth century, they immediately set about satisfying the demands of both high and low in spectacle. From the Christmas crib and the Holy Sepulchre emerged the first dramatic performances in church, which soon developed into morality plays on improvised stages and in public places. The dramatizations of the martyrs' lives and the allegorical plays with their combination of ancient mythology and Christian heroism became more and more ambitious. In the autumn of 1620 the Jesuit College opened its own

75

theatre with a play about St Pancras; in 1655, after some delay caused by the death of Ferdinand II, the University Theatre was opened with an auditorium that accommodated three thousand people and a stage capable of twelve to thirteen changes of scenery; a small room next to it was reserved for productions by students. From then on there were five or six major performances each year on public holidays, which were attended by members of the Imperial Court and therefore earned the designation 'ludi caesarei'. And in addition there were the 'spectacula divina', the 'spectacula publica', the 'spectacula privata' and the 'spectacula ambulantia' in the Jesuit theatres. The great painter Andrea del Pozzo, who decorated the University church, produced splendid stage-decorations. Father Nikolaus Avancinus made his début in 1640 with a play on St Francis Xavier and thereafter was the leading author of the Viennese Jesuits; he was a master of the rhetoric of the period, introduced great choirs and mass processions, dancing and combats; he filled his stage with martyrs and other saints, legendary and historic figures of all descriptions.

From 1665 German passages began to be interspersed with the Latin text and with the introduction of the vernacular, humour crept into Jesuit drama. Having acquired its Seneca, Vienna then produced its Plautus in the person of Johann Baptist Adolph, who made the figures on the Capitol dance, had riders mounted on goats and interpolated popular ditties. In the eighteenth century the Jesuit theatre lost its impetus; it found a successor in the school theatre of the Piarists' Schottengymnasium under Abbot Karl Fessler (1705–50), but in the meantime the secular theatre had also begun to branch out in all directions.

To celebrate the marriage of Leopold I and the Infanta Margareta in 1667 the Jesuit Father Francesco Sbarra devised a ballet for horses entitled 'La contesa dell' aria e dell' acqua' (The contest between air and water) and for the same occasion he wrote the libretto of an opera 'Il Pomo d'oro', which was finally produced for the Empress's birthday in 1668 after Burnacini's opera-house had been completed. It took the afternoons of 13th and 14th July to present the sixty-seven scenes in heaven, on earth and in the underworld with their lavish decorations, their costumes and a thousand actors. Burnacini devised the scenery (his designs have survived in magnificent engravings), while Marc' Antonio Cesti wrote the music, to which the Emperor Leopold contributed the duet for Cupid and Venus, and the dances were arranged by ballet-master Santo Venturi assisted by the head of the imperial armoury Agostino Santini. The magnificent décor and brilliant transformation-scenes of this production, which was repeated several times, were still spoken of long after the opera had ceased to be performed.

Any further development could only be achieved by concentrating on the drama and the music. Leading exponents of the neo-classical movement were the Italian poets Zeno and Metastasio, whose dramatic treatment of classical themes were set to music countless times throughout Europe. Charles VI succeeded in engaging both as court poets: Apostolo Zeno was resident in Vienna from 1718 to 1729 and was succeeded by Pietro Metastasio who lived in a house that still stands on the Michaelerplatz, a universally admired figure, until he died there in 1782.

In the eighteenth century the Viennese theatre, protected by the court and the nobility, retained its cosmopolitan character. One could hear French, Italian and Spanish as well as German spoken in the imperial palace. Members of society also employed foreign languages, principally French, in their amateur theatricals. The nobility, who had gathered at the Imperial Court, were a varied mixture of German, Slav, Hungarian, Italian, Lorraine and Netherland families.

Once the splendid though temporary wooden constructions of Burnacini and Galli-Bibiena had disappeared they were replaced by the two buildings which housed the Court Theatre until the present buildings were erected on the Ring: the old Burgtheater and the Kärntnertor Theatre.

The theatre on the bastion of the Kärntnertor was built in 1708. To begin with it was taken over by an Italian company, but from 1712 onwards it was run by the famous 'Hanswurst' Stranitzky, his successor Prehauser and the no less popular Bernardon. After a fire the building was renovated by the court architect Pacassi and with the opening performance of 7 July 1763 it began its new career as an opera house and theatre. Meanwhile, in 1741, when playing ball was clearly no longer fashionable, the 'Ball-house' next to the Burg had been converted into a theatre. Here it was mostly operas that were produced to begin with under the direction of Josef Karl Sellier. German drama had not yet become presentable at court. In 1747 a 'straight' play was produced for the first time in the Burgtheater which by contrast with the popular extempore comedies was based on a script.

Maria Theresa, who built the Schönbrunn Palace theatre in 1744–49, shared the interest of her court in the theatre but with reservations and she subjected it to strict rules of morality. In 1752 when the court in conjunction with the municipality of Vienna took over both theatres under its own direction, she issued instructions that no other compositions save those that emanated from the French or Italian or Spanish theatres were to be presented, that local comedies by Bernardon and others were to be dropped from the repertoire and no *double entendres* or dirty words were to be permitted. This decree, which virtually established the Viennese stage censorship, was due in no small part to the Empress's anger at an offensive remark made by Bernardon.

The Court Theatre now came under the control of the 'Music Count' Giacomo Conte Durazzo, a protégé of the Chancellor, Prince Kaunitz, who had come to Vienna as Genoese Ambassador and was appointed General Director of Productions. He pursued his own particular theatre policy with passionate single-mindedness, although everything he did was naturally subject to the imperial *placet*. The Burgtheater, now called the 'Théâtre français près de la cour', was taken over by a French company, while the theatre at the Kärntnertor produced mainly opera, ballet and such German drama as had survived. Durazzo engaged the composer Gluck for the French theatre in 1754 and reached an agreement with Favart, the famous writer of comedies, in Paris to supply comedies of his own and by other contemporary authors, which were then set to music in Vienna and converted into what we today call operettas.

After Durazzo's departure Josef von Sonnenfels, the grandson of a Berlin Rabbi, was appointed censor and exercised a decisive influence on the Court Theatres. Italian opera continued to flourish and under the ballet-masters Hilverding, and Gaspare and Domenico Angiolini ballet acquired a high reputation, culminating in the sensational first production by the brilliant choreographer Noverre together with Giovanni Vestris of 'L'Apothéose de Hercule' on 10 September 1767. The French company under Kaunitz's patronage was dissolved in 1772. But meanwhile earnest negotiations had been going on with Lessing, the first outstanding exponent of the new German drama, to persuade him to move to Vienna. He finally paid a visit in 1775 and was received several times by the Emperor, but his scepticism regarding the Viennese character remained.

Joseph II, who in other branches of government was still very much under his mother's thumb, found an outlet for his reforming zeal in the theatre, which he proposed to elevate to the status of a moral institution. The Court Theatre, renamed the 'German National Theatre', was instructed that 'from now on nothing but good, recognized originals and proper translations shall be performed'. From 1777 onwards

VIII St Peter's Church with its ornate stucco decoration executed by Italian artists in the first half of the eighteenth century

78

The old Burgtheater

not merely drama but also operettas, operas and ballets were again presented on both stages, and the Emperor had a special law promulgated to govern the theatre. In 1781 the actor Friedrich Ludwig Schröder was offered a star salary to move from Hamburg and the following year German 'Singspiel' scored a special triumph with a production of 'Il Seraglio' in the Burgtheater.

A detailed study of the development and constant regrouping of the Court Theatres at management level is not possible here. For some time the actor Franz Brockmann occupied a leading position. Towards the end of the century the successful dramatist Kotzebue, who had settled in Vienna, exercised a major influence on the drama. As a rule he staged the premières of his own gigantic productions either in Vienna or in Berlin, but he also played a part in the Burgtheater productions and at the same time wrote critiques of the performances for the court journal. From 1794 to 1806 the banker von Braun had a lien on all 'spectacles' and when he surrendered it on financial grounds, a 'Company of Cavaliers' was formed, with Prince Nicolaus Esterházy, Haydn's patron, as president, to keep the Court Theatres and also the 'Theater an der

Wien' going. But Count Palffy, who was in charge of drama, was soon carrying the entire reponsibility at great personal sacrifice to himself.

In November 1810 the two Court Theatres, which had frequently exchanged productions, were divorced from one another: the Burgtheater finally became the home of German drama, while the theatre at the Kärntnertor concentrated on opera and ballet. Not the least of the services Palffy rendered was to engage in 1814 a man who, although on paper he occupied a subordinate post, was to become one of the greatest theatre-directors of all time: this was Joseph Schreyvogel who built up the almost legendary reputation of the Burgtheater in Vienna as a leading German theatre.

The stock item even of the distinguished Burgtheater's repertoire was the international conversation-piece: the theatre also adapted itself to the powerful new literary trends. Between translations from the French there were exciting productions of the Weimar classics with such actors as Sophie Schröder and Heinrich Anschütz, and the old cultural links with Spain were revived with Schreyvogel's own translations of Calderón. But most significant was the introduction of native authors such as Bauernfeld, Friedrich Halm and, above all, Grillparzer, who wrote in his moving obituary of Schreyvogel in 1832:

'The whole field of dramatic art lay before him like a map of the world, or rather like a world, for there was life in his embrace. Indeed, so inexhaustible was the spring of love in his breast that, after the whole had been permeated, there was still enough warmth, even a glow left for the smallest details, that casting and stage-décor, the stress to be laid on a certain passage, the expression and deportment of the actors in a piece he had seen a hundred times were problems he approached with a mind as fresh as if it had never cherished bigger things, and no boy visiting the theatre for the first time was a more appreciative audience than he.'

In 1832, in one of those crises that are endemic to theatre life, Schreyvogel was the victim of a court intrigue, was dismissed and died soon after. His immediate successors were overshadowed both by him and by the outstanding personality of Eduard von Bauernfeld who followed them in controlling the destinies of the Burgtheater. Grillparzer's friend and a master of Viennese comedy, whose 'Leichtsinn aus Liebe' in 1831 proved to be one of the most successful productions at the Burgtheater, von Bauernfeld wrote of the Viennese Court Theatre during the so-called pre-March (1848) period and of its public: 'The fame of the Court Theatre regarding the so-called conversation piece, also where modern works are concerned, is undisputed . . .

The Kärntnertor Theatre of 1763–1868

Vienna has the good fortune to possess a large, theatre-loving public, which is not yet too critical and is in consequence appreciative – the most appreciative in the whole of Germany.'

The censorship, which watched over the morals of State and Church more closely than ever, saw to it that the tragedies were occasionally given an involuntary touch of light relief. For example, a priest was not allowed to appear on the stage, the word 'temple' was substituted for 'church', and Franz Moor and Ferdinand became their fathers' nephews!

Apart from the Court Theatre, the Kärntnerthor Theatre also gained a reputation as one of the leading opera-houses in Europe. Milder-Hauptmann, Beethoven's first Leonora, who was discovered by Schikaneder at the Theater an der Wien, and the young Henriette Sontag both had outstanding successes here; not only Italian but also French operas were performed; Cherubini was acclaimed; but the young German opera also scored a resounding success with 'Der Freischütz', and Carl Maria von Weber made a personal appearance with his 'Euryanthe'. And at the Kärntnertor ballet continued to enjoy tremendous popularity with Maria Taglioni performing as prima ballerina in 1822–24 and Fanny Elssler in 1844–47.

Meanwhile an equally popular form of theatrical performance had emerged in the suburbs, which presented the Viennese with a more down-to-earth image of themselves in their own vernacular. Impromptu comedy with its jokes and its uninhibited, salty humour found a particularly appreciative audience in the Danubian capital.

Joseph Anton Stranitzky, born in Graz in 1676, started presenting his 'Hanswurst' sketches at the Kärntnertor Theatre in 1712 and his audiences embraced all classes of society. Lady Montague saw an Amphitryon parody there in 1717 and wrote that, although she could not understand much of what was said, 'I have never laughed so much in all my life.' On 26 August Stranitzky presented Gottfried Prehauser (1699–1769) as his successor in the role of Hanswurst. Under the puritanical Maria Theresa the popular comedian was forced out into the suburbs, where he flourished more abundantly than ever. In addition to Hanswurst, other comic characters made their appearance and were so popular that they dominated the entire repertoire until well into the nineteenth century.

In 1737 the twenty-year-old Felix von Kurz (1717–84) joined Prehauser's company and built up a secondary character called Bernardon into a leading comic part which he continued to play for the rest of his life: first the simple locksmith's apprentice or foolish young student, then on to hilarious variations of the artful dodger and finally as he grew older, to the no less popular, more mature role of 'Father Bernardon'. His versatility was unlimited: on one occasion he played Mercury, Apollo, a juggler, a Styrian peasant, a Swabian snail-vendor, a Hussar, a Pole, a Croat, a shoemaker and an astrologer in one and the same piece.

In the next generation the theatre in Leopoldstadt, founded by Karl von Marinelli in 1781, became the home of popular comedy. The character 'Kasperl' invented by Johann Laroche (1745–1806) became so popular the quarter-crown which was charged for entry became known as a Kasperl. And in 1813 Adolf Bäuerle introduced in the 'Citizens of Vienna' a character called Staberl, who was played by the actor and manager Carl von Bernbrunn, known as Carl Carl, not only in the original play but also in many other pieces, including some by Nestroy. Even the popular theatre had finally gone over to scripted plays or sketches, although they still provided ample opportunity for extempore contributions, and during his sixteen years as resident author of the Leopoldstadt Theatre the industrious Bäuerle wrote seventy comedies,

J. A. Stranitzky, creator of
'Hanswurst' on the stage in Vienna

Nestroy also played Hanswurst as one
of his many roles, in this case in
'Der Doctor Nolens Volens' 1760
with Mad. Rohrbeck as Columbine

From the *Viennese Theatrical Journal* of 1842

several of which were set to music by Wenzel Müller and repeated many times. Vienna and the Viennese themselves were the most common theme, singing the praises of the city, making fun of its citizens.

But the general public wanted not merely to laugh and sing but also to revel in the whole fairy-tale atmosphere which the theatre had to offer, and, just as the Jesuits had taken to their plays about martyrs, the court to its mythological operas, so the suburban audiences were captivated by the new composite art-form of the magic farce with all its tricks and transformations. With increasing prosperity and education the demands made on both text and music became more exacting, and two actor-playwrights had already appeared, who were to give Viennese popular comedy an international reputation. Ferdinand Raimund transformed the stage into a world of fantasy and fable and not only made the Viennese laugh at his jokes but also touched their hearts. Johann Nepomuk Nestroy's first success was in the part of Sarastro, after which he proceeded to play eight hundred and seventy-eight other parts as a singer and an actor and in addition wrote eighty plays, most of which were set to music by Adolf Müller.

Nestroy was also a master of Viennese parody, who paved the way for Offenbach. A love of persiflage was part of the Viennese addiction to the theatre and special performances in the court theatres were often followed by hilarious skits in the suburban theatre. Sometimes there was lively competition between the Leopoldstadt and Josefstadt theatres to outdo one another in parodying the same performance in the Burgtheater, at the Kärntnertor or 'Auf der Wieden'.

Apart from Marinelli's theatre in Leopoldstadt, which was later taken over by Carl Carl, and the Josefstadt Theatre opened by 'Hanswurst' Karl Mayer in 1788, the 'Theater auf der Wieden' played a special role and for a time was under the same direction as the Court Theatre. By virtue of its position and of the fact that it was primarily given over to light entertainment, it was bracketed with the suburban theatres, but every now and then it was also chosen for artistic productions of the very highest quality.

On 14 October 1787, with imperial approval, the Principal, Christian Rossbach, had opened a theatre in the 'Freihaus' of Prince Starhemberg; a year later he had to surrender the lease to Johann Friedel who in turn sold it to Frau Schikaneder, in search for a theatre for her husband. On 12 July 1789 the highly versatile Emanuel Schikaneder began his career as an actor-manager with the opera 'Der dumme Anton

The programme for the first performance of 'The Magic Flute'

im Gebirge' by Schack and Gerl, and on 29 September 1791 his own opera, 'The Magic Flute' had its first performance to music composed, as was casually mentioned on the programme, by Herr Mozart. Schikaneder also added to Vienna's gallery of comic figures with his performance of Papageno, a character that was to outlive all the others. Sixty-seven days after the first performance of the opera, which he himself had conducted, the composer died, his work by then safely launched on its triumphal career. By the end of 1799 it had already been performed 214 times, and it has continued to delight not only the Viennese, but the entire world ever since. It combined everything the Viennese theatre had to offer: brilliant changes of scenery and stage-décor, warmth and humour.

At the turn of the century Schikaneder commissioned the court architect Rosenstängel to build a new stage with a bigger auditorium. The 'Theater an der Wien', as it was now called, thus became, and for a long time remained, the largest and technically most efficient theatre in Vienna. The first and second versions of Beethoven's 'Fidelio' both had their not very successful premières here, impressive subscription-concerts were organized, and Beethoven himself lived for a time in one of the 'Freihaus' buildings. All that remains today to remind us of that heroic period is the classical north façade with the Papageno group over the door.

Count Palffy, following the reconstruction work which he undertook in 1812, was able to indulge his passion for lavish stage productions; his children's ballets were particularly popular, until the performances were banned in order to protect the young female performers from the attentions of the Viennese men-about-town. In 1827 Carl Carl took over, forming with Wenzel Scholz and Johann Nestroy a memorable trio of comedians; in 1845 he was succeeded by Franz Pokorny with Albert Lortzing as conductor, and in 1848, the year of the revolution, the theatre was renamed the 'German National Theatre' (until 1852). From 1862 under Stampfer's direction the fairy-tale play became the vogue; in 1864 Josephine Gallmeyer was engaged and an exclusive contract was signed with Jacques Offenbach, thus assuring for the Theater an der Wien pride of place in the field of operetta.

IX Springtime in the Stadtpark, one of several public gardens surrounding the inner city

1848: Year of tumult

For centuries Vienna had been the residence of the Emperor, who claimed to be the direct successor of the Roman Cæsars and whose supremacy even outside his own domains was acknowledged by other Western rulers, head of the motley collection of German states and at the same time absolute ruler over the family of peoples, only some of whom belonged to the German Empire, in the hereditary Habsburg domains. In the nineteenth century, however, the Emperor of Austria was but one of several European emperors.

The revolutionary movement which started in Paris awakened the whole of Europe not only to the ideals of democracy but also to the idea of nationalism, which became a force in its own right and a direct challenge to the ruling dynasties. The watchword of German nationhood was first heard in the wars of liberation, spread to Vienna, and in the stormy year 1848 it suddenly burst into the open with surprising force. It confronted the Habsburg Empire with an insoluble problem and wrought a fundamental change in the character of the Habsburg capital.

The years and decades before March 1848 have become known as the 'pre-March' period, as if the entire epoch had merely led up to this moment when history gave its verdict. And indeed one does not have to look far for signs of a slowly-mounting tide of unrest, suggesting that the days of bigoted, reactionary absolutism were numbered. On the other hand, to recognize these signs in retrospect is also to recognize that this is not the whole truth, more especially in Vienna which wallowed in music, fable and farce.

The 'pre-March' intellectuals took every opportunity they could find to slip through the censor's net and to convey to the man-in-the-street, by way of the stage. and printed matter of every description, their dissatisfaction with the régime which they expressed so openly in conversation. One of the boldest of these critics was Anton Alexander Count Auersperg, who wrote under the pseudonym of Anastasius Grün and whose *Spaziergänge eines Wiener Poeten* (Rambles of a Viennese Poet) appeared in 1830/31.

The example of the enlightened emperor Joseph II is constantly invoked by these seekers after freedom, for his reforms, ephemeral as they were, had anticipated many of their demands and furthermore he was a 'German' emperor. At the same time, the fourth estate of the proletariat was emerging in the suburbs and Karl Beck, a native of Hungary, reflected a growing social awareness in his poem *Im wilden Quartier* (In the wild quarter) (1846). And the sentiments of the poet were voiced even more bluntly by the political thinker and agitator Friedrich Engels in the *Deutsche Brüsseler Zeitung* (German newspaper in Brussels) early in 1848:

'"I and Metternich will live to see it through," said the late lamented Emperor Franz I. If Metternich does not wish to give his emperor the lie, then he must die as soon as possible.

'The chequered, ill-begotten Austrian monarchy, this organized jumble of ten languages and nations, this incoherent compound of the most irreconcilable customs and laws is at last beginning to fall apart.

'The honest German citizen has for years paid his tribute of admiration to the director of this stagnating state-machine, the cowardly rogue and assassin Metternich.

'If old Metternich does not soon take the same road as his "trusty" Franz, he may still live to see how the imperial monarchy, which he has so laboriously held together, collapses and, for the most part, falls into the hands of the bourgeois; he may yet experience the unspeakable, when the "bourgeois tailors" and "bourgeois grocers" no longer take off their hats to him in the Prater but call him simply Herr Metternich. A few more upheavals, a few more bills for armaments and Charles Rothschild will have bought up the entire Austrian monarchy.

'We look forward to the victory of the bourgeoisie over Austrian imperialism with genuine pleasure. Our only wish is that it should be really common, really dirty, really Jewish bourgeois who buy up this ancient and revered empire. Such a nauseating horse-whipping, paternalistic, lousy government deserves to go down to a truly lousy, shaggy-haired, stinking adversary. Herr Metternich can rest assured that, when the time comes, we shall delouse this adversary just as mercilessly as he will be deloused by him before long.'

In March 1848 all the stories that had been going the rounds of the 'Beisls' and coffee-houses suddenly became harsh reality. The Lower Austrian Estates met on the 13th in the Ständehaus. The city was alive with rumours, an excited mob rushed through the Herrengasse, shots were fired and there were forty-four dead. A delegation of citizens demanded Metternich's dismissal; apparently unperturbed, he issued a statement that he did not want to be held responsible for further bloodshed and would therefore resign.

On the 15th a liberal constitution was drafted. Ferdinand the Kind drove through the city in an open carriage and was warmly applauded. Government after government fell and in each successive Cabinet the tug-of-war continued. The workers and students demonstrated again on 15 May, demanding: 'Only one Chamber! The closest ties with Germany!' On 25 May barricades were erected in the streets in protest against the dissolution of the Academic Legion, and the decree was rescinded. A Citizen's Security Committee was set up.

On 15 June the feeble-minded Ferdinand appointed the Archduke Johann his deputy.

On 9 July Richard Wagner arrived in Vienna on his flight from Dresden to Zurich and sent his wife Minna an enthusiastic account of the situation, assuming that the revolutionaries he supported had already succeeded:

'. . . Vienna, on which I first set my eyes again on a fine bright Sunday enchanted me – I admit it! I found Paris again, only more beautiful, more gay and German. During the sixteen years that have passed since I last saw Vienna the whole city has been renewed: its half million inhabitants, all dressed in German colours, poured through the streets on Sunday as if in celebration – on the Saturday a wavering, incompetent Ministry had been forced out by the People's Committee! You should see the faces of these people: everything that disgusts you in the people of Dresden would appeal to you here. The National Guard in fairly military dress with broad silk, tricolour sashes: the students (8000) stand guard in old German frock-coats with top-hats on their heads and carrying muskets and sabres: I have seen almost nothing but fine people. And now this opulence! This life! The strange costumes the women wear, an entirely new type of hat with feathers and tricolour German hat-bands. On almost every house a German flag. Then the public criers, men, women and children: "Fall of the Pillersdorf Ministry!" one farthing. "The Americans will not abandon the Germans!" one farthing. "Declare war on the Russians!" one farthing. "Final collapse of the aristocracy!" one farthing. And so it goes on. But everything is gay, calm and youthful . . .'

On 22 July a Reichstag based on universal suffrage met in the Riding School. On 6 October the storm broke again: War Minister Latour was lynched and then strung up on a lamp-post; people stormed into the centre of the town from the suburbs. Polish

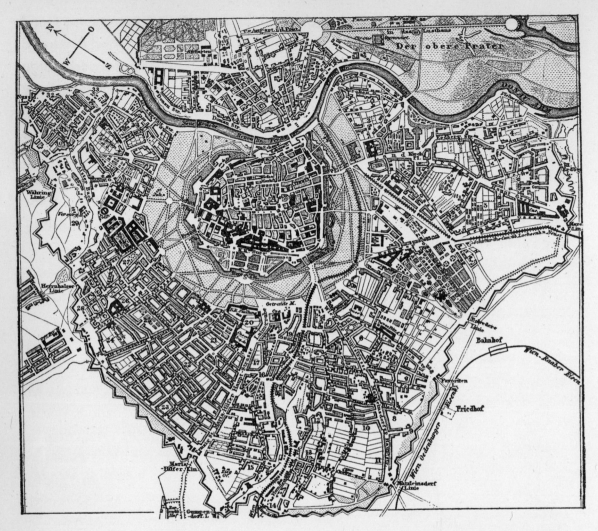

'Plan of the Imperial Capital Vienna' before the construction of the Ring, in Meyer's
Conversations–Lexicon of 1853

troops defended the arsenal but abandoned it to the mob the following day. A civilian
Free Corps was formed under the command of Cäsar Wenzel Messenhauser.

In the meantime, however, the representatives of the former ruling caste had not
been idle. Field-Marshal Prince Windischgrätz, whom the Emperor had appointed
his *alter ego*, surrounded the city with his troops. The civilian defenders were no
match for the army, most of which consisted of non-German troops, and by 31
October the city had fallen to the Field-Marshal.

Robert Blum and Julius Fröbel, the two deputies of the Frankfurt Parliament who
had arrived in Vienna, were arrested. Blum was shot, but the life of his companion, a

nephew of the kindergarten Fröbel, was spared. In his pocket a document was found which aroused the excited interest of the Town Commandant. In it Fröbel developed his arguments in favour not of a pan-German solution but of an Austrian federation of Danubian states which was presumably based on the Swiss Confederation where he had spent so many years.

With this one exception the courts martial showed no mercy: Messenhauser and the two 'radical' journalists Becker and Jellinek were all shot.

On 2 December Ferdinand the Kind, who had fled to Olmütz with his court, abdicated in favour of his nephew Franz Joseph. The eighteen-year-old Emperor knelt before his uncle to receive his blessing. 'Courage, my boy! It was done gladly,' said Ferdinand and stroked his cheek.

The era of Franz Joseph

The steam had gone out of the revolution and everything seemed as before. Vienna had an emperor again, who could appear in public. When he did, it was always in his new general's uniform and he became known as the 'red-trousered lieutenant'. When Queen Victoria met him, she said: 'I like the young Emperor, I must admit; there is much spirit and boldness in his warm blue eyes, and he shows a certain agreeable gaiety, when the occasion arises. He is slender and graceful, and even in the mêlée of dancers and archdukes, all in uniform, he can always be recognized as their head. There is a certain something about him that lends authority.'

Franz Joseph was convinced that he had a mission 'to protect the people by sternness and prudence against the temptations of revolution'. He frequently appeared in the imperial box at the Burgtheater and never failed to notice when one of the actors fluffed his lines.

It was a time of growing responsibility and mounting anxiety for him; he was faced by formidable adversaries in the power-game of European politics. The Habsburg empire was crumbling in the west and the south; first the Netherlands, then the possessions on the Rhine and in Italy were lost and the losses had to be made good at the expense of the sick man on the Bosphorus and the Slav kingdoms which emerged from his European inheritance. The monarchy, which, after the Congress of Vienna, covered some 250,000 square miles, expanded until 1908 to as much as 270,000 square miles. The two pillars of imperial power, the Army and the Church, seemed indestructible. The aged Metternich had returned from his exile in England to his palace on the Rennweg and, until his death in 1859, remained the Emperor's oracle. The Concordat of 1855 reinforced the power of the confessional and the constitution which had been conceded before the initial shock of the March revolution had worn off was no longer even mentioned.

But 'Josephinism' was by no means dead in Vienna and the flame of the nineteenth century was still licking at the old foundations. Liberalism was creeping into even the topmost strata of government, the Constitution of 1861 created the framework for a constitutional monarchy and, despite the protests of Pius IX and the determined

96

opposition of the Cardinal Archbishop of Vienna, Rauscher, the Concordat gave way to the Liberal legislation of 1868. The expansion of trade and industry strengthened the position of the middle class and replaced the hierarchical social structure of the past with the pluralism of the new age.

This new era also brought far-reaching changes in the city itself. In the Napoleonic wars Vienna had already ceased to be a defensible fortress. The old bastions had become meaningless and in fact the events of 1848 had brought it home to the government that they could even be an obstacle when dealing with civil disorder. In order to make it easier to control the suburbs, barracks were built to act as forts and a gigantic arsenal, a fortress in itself, was constructed. In December 1857 the Emperor issued a decree to open up the Ring, the first paragraph of which read as follows:

'It is My Will that the extension of the inner city of Vienna, with regard to its appropriate connection with the suburbs, should be taken in hand as soon as possible, and that consideration should be given to the regulation and embellishment of My Residence and Capital at the same time. For this purpose I give My permission to abolish the circumvallation and fortifications of the Inner City, as well as the surrounding ditches.'

This unique town-planning project was set in motion with commendable caution. The finest architects of the day were invited to compete. The result was the 'Ring' which with its green open spaces and official buildings helped to create the image of Vienna that leaves such an indelible impression on the modern visitor. It was a remarkably successful marriage between the Gothic of the cathedral and the Baroque of the churches and palaces on the one hand and, on the other, the eclecticism of a new industrial age which had not yet fully evolved its own style.

Before the emergence of the Ring, the Votivkirche had been built to commemorate an unsuccessful attempt on the life of the young Emperor. Designed by Heinrich von Ferstel and modelled closely on the French Gothic, its graceful twin spires dominate the Ring at the Schottentor and might well serve as a Biedermeier-style décor for Schiller's *Maid of Orleans*. The monumental Town Hall is also well endowed with Gothic arches and towers. And next to the medieval seat of city government stands the severely classical State Parliament, a temple fronted by a statue of Pallas Athene.

All the other buildings in the Ring were modelled on the Renaissance. Ferstel, architect of the Gothic Votivkirche, built the new University in the Renaissance style, and Hansen, architect of the classical Parliament building, adopted the same style in his Academy of Fine Arts. Siccardsburg and van der Nüll won the competition for the construction of the new Opera House at the Kärntnertor. A decisive influence was also exercised by Gottfried von Semper, whose designs were well ahead of his time. This famous architect, who was then a Professor at the Polytechnikum in Zurich, had been asked to approve the designs submitted for the court museums by Hansen, Ferstel, Löhr and Hasenauer; he was finally invited to carry the projects through and chose Hasenauer's plan as the basic design. In October 1871 he came to Vienna at the Emperor's invitation, his ambition being to build a spacious forum such as he had already planned for Dresden: a number of triumphal arches and porticoes were to link the New Imperial Palace with the Museums. While Hasenauer was busy working on the World Exhibition, his design for the new Burgtheater was elaborated by Semper. After Semper's death (1879) Hasenauer was left in sole charge of all these buildings, including the New Imperial Palace (Neue Hofburg).

This was a period in which people seemed largely unaware of the economic and social changes going on around them and lived in the past to a degree unknown before. Monuments were erected and not only the rulers and generals but also the great poets and composers were honoured like kings. The day had finally passed when princely dilettantes and their court composers would give a special performance of a Handel Oratorio merely to provide leaven for contemporary compositions. The appeal of the old masters was unchallenged. A new, anonymous audience emerged; Press criticism came into its own as an opinion-moulder. The tireless wit and irony of Saphir in Bäuerle's theatrical journal and in the periodical *Der Humorist* was followed by the unrelieved gravity and the professionalism of a Hanslick, for whom the solidity of Brahms, the Hamburger, has so much more appeal than the gigantomachy of of Wagner, the Saxon.

At the meetings of the 'Society of the Friends of Music' Beethoven constituted the focal point; was, one might even say, an object of worship. The Court Kapellmeister, Otto Nicolai, composer of the enchanting opera 'The Merry Wives of Windsor', founded the Philharmonic concerts with the court opera orchestra in 1842, and for the first time the masterpieces which Haydn, Mozart and Beethoven had thrown on the market with such abandon were played by professional musicians who had carefully rehearsed them. Whereas Beethoven had had only two rehearsals for the first performance of his Ninth Symphony and his musicians made such a mess of the second movement that they had to start again, Nicolai had thirteen rehearsals for the same

X Picking grape in the Nussberg vineyard besid the Danub Canal nea Grinzin

X NUSSBERG

work. So exacting a musician as Berlioz, who conducted the leading orchestras of Europe on his tours, wrote after his appearance as a guest-conductor in Vienna in 1845: 'The concerts which Nicolai organizes and conducts in the Redoutensaal are worthy counterparts of our concerts in the Paris Conservatoire. Here I heard a scene from "Oberon", the aria "Unis dès la plus tendre enfance" from "Iphigenia in Tauris", a beautiful symphony by Nicolai and the wonderful, incomparable symphony in C minor by Beethoven. All this was rendered with that profound fidelity, that perfection of detail and that powerful over-all effect which, at least for me, when performed by such an orchestra, represent the finest product of modern art, the truest manifestation of what we today call "La Musique" . . .' Every year a Nicolai Concert is still held to commemorate the founder of the world-famous Vienna Philharmonic.

Against the monumental background of Viennese classicism new generations were competing for a place in the enormous Museum of Music that was under construction. Symphony after symphony was composed, each striving to carry on where Beethoven had left off. Berlioz displayed the brilliant colours of the modern orchestra, Brahms settled in Vienna, Bruckner realised his symphonic virtuosity of a Paganini or a Liszt.

In the city which had heard 'Figaro' and 'The Magic Flute' for the first time, the masters of German opera were also anxious to vindicate themselves. In the wake of Carl Maria von Weber the Mecklenburg composer von Flotow had a triumphal first performance of his 'Martha'. Conradin Kreutzer from Messkirch, Louis Spohr from Brunswick and Albert Lortzing from Berlin all performed as Kapellmeister for stage productions. The highly successful operatic premières of Méhul, Auber, Boieldieu, Halévy, Meyerbeer and Bizet in Paris were usually followed immediately by performances in Vienna, and the rising young star in the Italian operatic firmament, Giuseppe Verdi, made a personal appearance in Vienna when his 'Nabucco' was performed. Richard Wagner, who had written a *Pilgrimage to Beethoven* and an article on the Viennese court opera, also sought to win the approval of the musical metropolis; his critics, however, succeeded in preventing the première of 'Tristan and Isolde', which had been planned for 1861, and the Viennese heard the exciting new strains of this opera for the first time at the Augarten concerts, where the indefatigable Johann Strauss conducted excerpts from all three acts.

In the field of drama, Schreyvogel had built up a remarkable reputation for the Burgtheater which was not easy to maintain. Constant changes at the administrative level encouraged the sort of rivalries and intrigues which the Viennese had always indulged in; with His Imperial Majesty as final arbiter in the background, senior court officials, the Finance Minister and the Intendant General, the Artistic Director and the Treasurer of the Court Theatres, the Council of Management and even specially privileged actors all had a say in the running of the theatre. Among them were Count Moritz Dietrichstein, who drew up regulations for the court actors and founded the Council of Management, the autocratic Count Czernin, the easy-going Professor of Aesthetics Deinhardstein, and the somewhat effete poet Franz von Holbein. In contemporary literature, apart from the universally respected but rather elusive Grillparzer, the leading figures were the dramatist Friedrich Halm (Eligius Freiherr Muench-Bellinghauser) and the playwright Eduard von Bauernfeld. The most eloquent spokesman of a period that was plagued by new problems was Friedrich Hebbel, who found in the actress Christine Enghaus, chief rival of the popular Julie Rettich, not merely the ideal life-companion but also a brilliant interpreter. For in Vienna it was not just the plays that drew people to the theatre; actors outshone politicians in the popularity stakes. Life without crises in the theatre was apt to become boring.

In April 1849 one of those plays which inspire fresh confidence in the vitality of youth succeeded in passing the censorship. This was 'Die Karlsschüler' by Heinrich Laube from Silesia, who had previously been a liberal deputy in the German National Assembly and a spokesman of German youth. After the curtain had fallen, Laube made an impromptu speech to the enthusiastic audience at the Burgtheater. The same year, after his qualifications had been duly considered, he was made Director of the Court Theatre. Although he himself was an author, like his predecessor Schreyvogel, he was more interested in the theatre than in literature. 'In the present day stage-production must exercise a creative power of its own, otherwise two thirds of the modern plays cannot survive.' His not very high opinion of contemporary German dramatists was also reflected in the fact that, like other Viennese theatre-directors before him, he preferred to look to Paris for his plays, for the brilliant dialogue of contemporary French playwrights seemed to him superior, even in translation, to that of the average German. He regarded cultivation of the spoken word as much more important than scene-setting; that is why an enormous amount of work was done under Laube at relatively little cost. He was the most economical of the great directors. Actors in his team became almost legendary figures: Sonnenthal, Baumeister, Dawison, Lewinsky and Hartmann, and amongst the women Marie Seebach and Charlotte Wolter. In 1867 he quarrelled with Friedrich Halm, who had been promoted to Intendant General, over their respective responsibilities and resigned. In 1871 Laube reappeared in Vienna and spent nine highly successful years at the Municipal Theatre, which he had founded.

In the meantime a director of great artistic talent had taken over at the Burgtheater. The highly cultured Franz von Dingelstedt (1870–81) knew how to move the masses, once again paying more attention to scenery and drawing up a more ostentatious repertoire with Shakespeare as the main attraction. He suggested Brahms should write the music for Faust II. But Dingelstedt was no hothead; nor for that matter was his successor, the poet Adolf Wilbrandt, who produced his own translation of Sophocles and staged a performance of *Faust* spread over three evenings, only to retire six years later exhausted. For a time the direction was carried on by the star actor Sonnenthal, who was ennobled, and under him the ensemble moved into the splendid new building on the Ring.

In 1890 the court authorities engaged another outsider as artistic director of the Burgtheater in the person of the lawyer Max Burckhard who shortly before had transferred from the Judicature to the Ministry of Education and who on his own confession had only been inside a theatre six or seven times in his life. But his appointment, which looked almost like a practical joke, proved remarkably successful, for the new man was enthusiastic and without inhibitions; he attacked such hallowed institutions as the oligarchy of so-called producers; brought in such actors as Adele Sandrock, Friedrich Mitterwurzer and the fabulous Joseph Kainz with their new look and wider range of expression; introduced Ibsen, Gerhart Hauptmann and Sudermann to the repertoire; groomed Anzengruber and encouraged Schnitzler. Hermann Bahr referred to Burckhard as 'the strongest, broadest, most individual Austrian of his generation . . . He was the man who taught us to long for the experience of tragedy and only thanks to him were we ready for Mahler.'

When, after eight years, Burckhard returned to the Judicature in an administrative capacity, in order to help protect 'the individual against the beast of the State that threatens, crushes and devours all individuality', his place at the Burgtheater was filled by a 'literary' appointment that is still controversial: the critic Dr Paul Schlenther, who represented the naturalist trend for which Berlin had recently became so famous.

Katharina Schratt and
Heinrich Laube.
From *Kikeriki* 1884

One of the pillars of the Burgtheater was Katharina Schratt, who made a name for herself at the Municipal Theatre as a 'shrew' during Laube's directorship. As a society lady she represented all that was best in the Burgtheater tradition; in her professional capacity she had acquired impeccable manners and was accustomed to consorting on the stage with people of top quality – so why confine it to the theatre? The sensitive Empress Elisabeth, who was a Bavarian princess of sixteen when she married the rather wooden Franz Joseph, had never felt completely at home at the Viennese court and spent much of her time travelling. In the vivacious Schratt, who was separated from her husband, Baron Kiss von Itebe, the Empress thought she had found a suitable companion for her ageing husband, who had become increasingly absorbed in his State documents and military papers. So this strange friendship developed between Emperor and actress, who would visit one another, take long walks together in the park of Schönbrunn and exchange letters which became more and more tender without overstepping the bounds of mutual respect. But Schratt's devotion had its limits where her pride as an actress was involved. Schlenther did not find this immaculate society lady suitable for leading parts in plays by Ibsen and Hauptmann and all her connections availed her nothing: her imperial friend, the personification of moral probity, steadfastly refused to intervene with the Director and for quite a time Katharina was deeply hurt, despite the most moving, abject letters from Franz Joseph. This was the period when both of them missed the unselfish friendship of Elisabeth, who had been stabbed by an anarchist in Geneva.

Among all the rapidly expanding enterprises of the nineteenth century in industry, technology and science, it is the School of Medicine in Vienna which merits special mention. Its fame had already been established in the eighteenth century by Gerhard van Swieten, whom Kaunitz persuaded to move from Leyden to Vienna. Joseph II had given it his full support. The anthropologist Carl von Rokitansky, who had studied philosophy in Königgrätz, opened the Institute for Pathological Anatomy in 1862 on the understanding that there would be complete freedom for research. Joseph Skoda from Pilsen, a relative of the founder of the Skoda works, was a pioneer of diagnostics who developed the physical method of investigation. And Ferdinand von Hebra from Brünn discovered new methods of curing skin diseases. More controversial, although they were eventually accepted, were the theories of the Hungarian gynaecologist Ignaz Philipp Semmelweiss regarding the causes of puerperal fever. And finally Viennese surgery became world-famous thanks to Theodor Billroth, who moved from Zurich to Vienna in 1867 and who also became a familiar figure in Viennese musical circles: in his house the new works of his friend Johannes Brahms were tried out, and this extremely energetic scholar, already a considerable pianist, also learned to play the viola so that he could take a more active part in the soirées of chamber music.

The stormy year 1848 had merely been a phase, though a particularly important one, in the social revolution that lasted throughout the century. With the irresistible advance of democracy in public life, with the establishment of the third estate and the emergence of the fourth, and with the growth of a national consciousness with particular intensity among the Germans but also affecting the other racial communities in the monarchy, the underlying split in the imperial capital now became apparent with all its frightening implications: was it the first and the most German of German cities or the seat of a federation of Danubian nations? Was it to take the leading position in the new German Reich or merely to fulfil an Austrian mission in southeast Europe? And since Prussia's victory in 1866 the question could be put even more simply: Austria, or union with Germany?

With the triumph of liberalism in the 'sixties the new financial moguls took their place beside the hereditary nobility and played a substantial part in the social and cultural life. In the course of the century the Jewish element in the population grew from 1·5 to 14·15 per cent but influence on commercial and cultural life increased even more. In politics the lawyers with their Western ideas set the tone, free trade

Dr Cajetan Felder.
Caricature of 1884

was on everyone's lips, new industries sprang up, the city grew and its technical services expanded. In 1867 a law was passed granting freedom of association and political clubs and associations appeared, initially on a local basis in the various regions; an opposition group emerged in the City Council in 1875, in 1886 the first anti-semites were elected to the City Parliament and in 1900 the first Social Democrat deputies.

The leading exponent of the liberal era was the progressive Mayor Dr Cajetan Felder. During his period of office the regulation of the Danube was carried out, the first water-conduit system was constructed, local government reforms were introduced, the new Parliament Building erected, the Central Cemetery designed. In 1873 Vienna, following the example of London and Paris, held a World Exhibition which was larger than any of its predecessors. To further the cause of industry and trade princely receptions and social functions of all kinds were held which were reminiscent of the glittering displays of the Vienna Congress. But in the midst of the festivities a wave of financial speculation led to the collapse of the Stock Exchange and an economic crisis followed.

But, crisis or no crisis, the true spirit of Vienna was always to be found in music and the theatre. In addition to the gallant social comedy and classical tragedy of the Burgtheater and to the international repertoire of the court opera, the lighter muse was also being cultivated in the 'Auf der Wieden' theatre, in Josefstadt and Leopoldstadt, and in the new theatres which were appearing on the Ring. In addition to the concerts held in the 'Haus der Musikfreunde' and in the Bösendorff Hall which was opened in 1872, light music was penetrating from the suburbs into the heart of Vienna. The quartet formed by Josef Lanner and Johann Strauss (The Elder), which played special arrangements and potpourris until it moved on to original dance compositions,

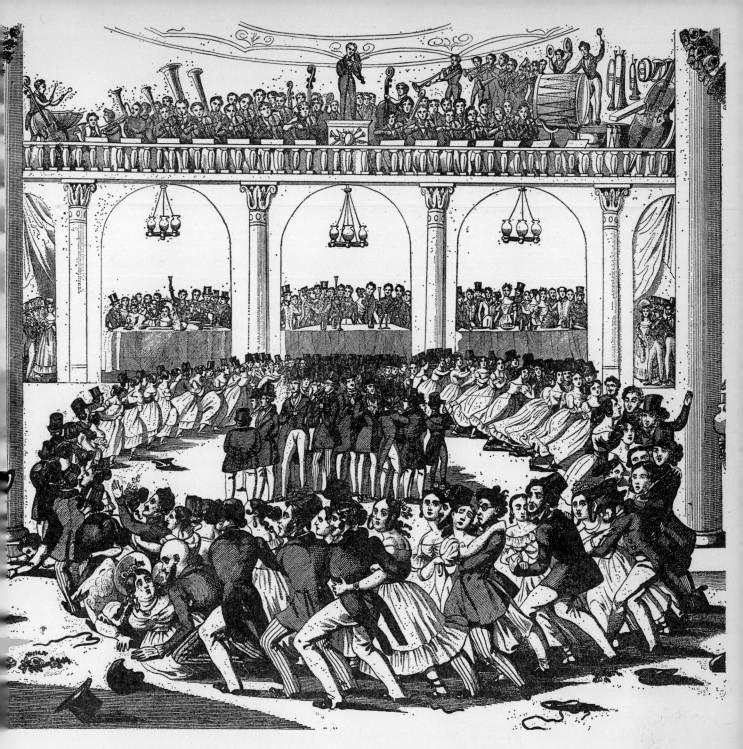

'The Grand Galop by Joh. Strauss', coloured engraving by A. Geiger in the *Viennese Theatrical Journal* of 26 June 1839, with an editorial gloss by Bäuerle: 'Strauss's (the Elder) Grand Galop has so electrified the dancing world that a pictorial representation of the energetic effect produced by this exciting music cannot be unwelcome. Everything takes on a life and movement of its own and reflects the gaiety which pervades the original composition'

paved the way for the 'salon orchestra' and 'Viennese ensemble'. Strauss in particular, who survived his friend and appeared in the Sperl amusement palace in Leopoldstadt, became a familiar figure in Vienna: 'Violin in hand, conducting like a man possessed, moved by invisible powers and yet as oracular as Pythia: hot-blooded as an African, with a lust for the sunshine of life, daringly modern, restless by nature, unattractively passionate' – such was Heinrich Laube's description of him. And his sons took after him; Johann Strauss the Younger, in particular, put even his famous father in the shade with his waltzes. Brahms and Bruckner were both admirers of this juggler with tunes, and Richard Wagner described him as 'the most musical head I have ever encountered'. On a visit to Vienna Offenbach whispered in the Waltz King's ear that operettas were even more profitable than waltzes and Strauss, competing with Franz von Suppé and Karl Millöcker, wrote one operetta after the other, finally composing the music to a libretto from Paris for his masterpiece, 'Die Fledermaus'. The comic operas of Favart with music by Gluck, the operas of Haydn, Dittersdorf and Mozart, the farces and parodies of Nestroy and Meisl for which Wenzel Müller and Adolf Müller composed so many couplets, all played their part in the birth of the Viennese operetta with its touch of Parisian elegance spiced with Hungarian paprika, Bohemian and Polish rhythms, but always with the underlying waltz-beat that was so peculiar to Vienna, weaving countless new melodies from the simple triple-time pattern and finally evolving from the infectious, quasi-demonic gaiety of Strauss into the sentimentality of Lehár with a nostalgic glance at grand opera, while in the cafés and at the Heurig Johann Schrammel with his clarinet quartet harked back to the folk-music of Lanner and Strauss.

Johann Strauss the Younger.
Viennese caricature of 1884

XI Tenement block on the Linke Wienzeile,
designed by Otto Wagner

From the Secession to the present day

The Emperor, that dignified, uniformed figure who had become a living monument, continued to live on. Jubilee followed jubilee: silver wedding, the golden jubilee of his reign, the diamond jubilee. And with the years the burden of office and of personal tragedy grew heavier: his son and heir shot himself; his brother, chosen to be Emperor of Mexico, was executed, his wife was stabbed, the second in succession to the throne murdered. At least the old man was spared the one thing that would have dealt the final blow after sixty-eight years of devoted service to the long family line: two years after he died at Schönbrunn, the proud Habsburg Empire collapsed.

The financial crisis of 1873, which claimed many victims among small people, destroyed any confidence that was left in the liberal leadership of the city of Vienna. In 1875 the 'Democrats' emerged as an opposition group in the City Council. Georg von Schönerer, who had been a Member of Parliament since 1873, started his pan-German movement, which was against the Habsburgs, against the Roman Catholic Church, against the Jews, against co-existence with the Slavs and in favour of unconditional union with Germany. In 1880 the 'Deutsche Schulverein' was formed and gained wide and enthusiastic support: its aim was to ensure the supremacy of the German language in the empire, although the population – leaving out Hungary – was only 35 per cent German-speaking. The oppressed Slavs, the liberals and the reactionary element in the Army found it necessary to join forces in a common defence against the pan-German movement. In January 1894 the imperial courts denied the non-German minorities in Vienna, most of them Czechs, the right to employ their own mother-tongue in their meetings and associations. In 1897 there was such a wave of indignation when the Badeni government conceded the use of Czech and Slovak as second official languages in Bohemia and Moravia that the government had to resign. The many Czechs who had found employment in the imperial capital were temporarily forbidden by the city authorities to have their own schools.

Dr Victor Adler, who was a general practitioner before he founded the Social Democratic Party of Austria, began as a fellow-traveller of Schönerer but was obliged by the latter's rabid anti-semitism to branch out on his own and was greatly influenced by his friend Friedrich Engels. On 1 May 1890 the first May procession of the proletariat took place in the Prater, where until then only the social élite had paraded in their carriages. In August 1892 Adler reported to Engels in London: 'Our people – Germans and Czechs – have brilliant qualities and only the damned Jesuitism of past centuries has made us appear lackeys and appendages of the European movement. The country's economic backwardness is disappearing, one can truthfully say, hourly.' It was to be one of Adler's chief aims to collaborate with the Czechs, in order to prevent the formation of a 'Young Czech–Russian–pan–Slav clique'. In March 1893 the tenth anniversary of Karl Marx's death was celebrated and on 11 September of the same year Friedrich Engels and August Bebel, who were both on a visit to Vienna, were given a special reception. Adler committed his party to achieving its aims by strictly legal methods but for the moment the existing electoral laws denied it adequate representation in either the municipal or the national parliament.

In the election of 1875 Karl Lueger (pronounced 'Lu-eger'), a doctor of law, became a member of the City Parliament and three years later he founded his own 'Wirtschaftspartei' ('Economic Party'), which eventually led to the formation of the Christian Social Party. In 1885, on an anti-liberal, anti-'Jewish plutocracy' ticket Lueger was elected by a bare majority to the Imperial Council and in the 1893 elections for the City Council, the municipal executive body, he succeeded at the third attempt in defeating Councillor von Goldschmidt. In 1895, when his way to the Mayor's office was barred by a hostile majority in the Council, the machinations of his opponents suddenly presented an opportunity of overcoming this obstacle but Lueger refused to take it and forced fresh elections for the City Parliament, which were fought with unprecedented ferocity. It was soon apparent that Lueger's demagogic talents gave him a marked superiority over his liberal opponents, who were not close to the masses and were known as the 'advocates'. His 'suburban' rhetoric had a wide appeal, especially as he knew how to exploit the grievances of the lower-middle-class. 'The Jewish Press has stirred up class hatred and international hatred. Once the Jews, who sow dissension between peoples for their own profit, have been conquered, then the national disputes will also cease . . .' His appeal to the workers was 'to crush the common enemy, liberalism'. But, speaking of their new party, he tried to adopt a more accommodating tone: 'In the negative sense Social Democracy may be right and I, like any other Catholic, must agree with it.'

Lueger after winning the election.
Kikeriki 30 March 1890

Lueger succeeded in inflicting a resounding defeat on the liberals, who for so long had had a commanding majority, and when, shortly after, another election was held, the alliance of Christian Social and German National parties emerged with an even bigger majority. Lueger was elected Mayor for the second time but the Emperor on the advice of his government refused to recognize his election; he also refused to ratify the third election and, when Lueger was elected a fourth time, intervened personally to persuade him not to accept office. But the Council was not to be browbeaten: the fifth election on 8 April 1897 was ratified by the Emperor eight days later.

The majestic, bearded 'handsome Karl' now emerged as not just a demagogue of genius but also as a tireless and intelligent administrator, to whom his Social Democrat successor under the First Republic, Karl Seitz, paid the following tribute:

'The Lueger era represents a great step forward towards transferring important means of production from the hands of private capital to the community, to a communal economy. It will be one of our major tasks to carry on and complete the work that Lueger began.'

While Lueger was alive, of course, the Socialists in the City Council protested publicly against 'the Byzantine orgies and against the idolatry which Lueger encourages around himself'. When the 'people's mayor' died on 10 March 1910, he was still in office in City Hall. In the vast funeral cortège the Emperor himself was present and Lueger was given the most pretentious tomb in the whole of Vienna: as you drive into the city today from the airport at Schwechat past the great Central Cemetery, you cannot fail to see the dome of the Mausoleum towering above the tombs of Vienna's great musicians, poets, actors and scholars. A Dr Karl Lueger Square and a Dr Karl Lueger monument are further reminders of the man who, as even the newspapers of his opponents admitted, 'had such a strange power over the Viennese'.

The turn of the century was not just the Lueger era, during which Adolf Hitler was incubating those ideas that were eventually to gain him a triumphal entry into a jubilant Vienna. There was another Vienna, which, in spite of all the anti-Semitic, pan-German polemics, still managed to retain the aura of a true imperial capital, cosmopolitan, multi-racial, pursuing in its own way its mission as a centre of German culture. If on the one hand the nineteenth century with its clash of generations, of social classes and of economic interests gave a discordant impression, on the other hand there was the astonishing unanimity with which men of the most diverse temperaments were able to agree on projects which looked well forward into the twentieth century. Architects and musicians, philosophers and doctors, poets and stage people, drawn together by visible and invisible bonds, could be seen in Vienna's coffee-houses. Hermann Bahr in his study of expressionism lists several names: 'Riegel (the art historian) had been at University since 1895 with Wiekhoff, discoverer of Julian-Flavian-Trajan art, at a time when Hugo Wolf was still alive, Burckhard was rejuvenating the Burgtheater, Mahler the opera, Hofmannsthal and Schnitzler were still young, the Secession was beginning, Otto Wagner was founding his school, Roller the graphic theatre, Olbrich, Hoffmann the Austrian arts and crafts, Adolf Loos appeared, Arnold Schönberg emerged, Reinhardt walked unknown through quiet streets dreaming of the future, Kainz came home, Weininger went up in flames, Ernst Mach held his popular scientific lectures, Joseph Popper wrote his *Phantasien eines Realisten* [Fantasies of a Realist] and Chamberlain, who had taken refuge from the distractions of the world in our gentle city, wrote the *Foundations of the 19th Century* . . .'

The list can be extended at will. In the house of the successful engineer and industrialist Karl Wittgenstein, where Brahms was a frequent visitor, his two sons were growing up: Paul, the well-known pianist, and Ludwig Josef Johann, who, after an eventful life as a philosopher, soldier, school teacher and monastery gardener, developed the 'Scientific Philosophy' which had been a product of the 'Vienna Circle' under Ernest Mach, and finally went to England where he became the leading exponent of a new school of philosophy. And from 1891 until 1938 Sigmund Freud lived at No. 19 Bergstrasse in the ninth district, where he laid the foundations of a new science. Then there was the famous feuilletonist Peter Altenberg, who turned the

Otto Wagner'
design for th
Church am Steinho
From the thir
volume of th
four-volume wor
by Otto Wagne
Einige Skizze
Projekte und au
geführte Bauwerk
which was publishe
by Schroll
Vienna in 19

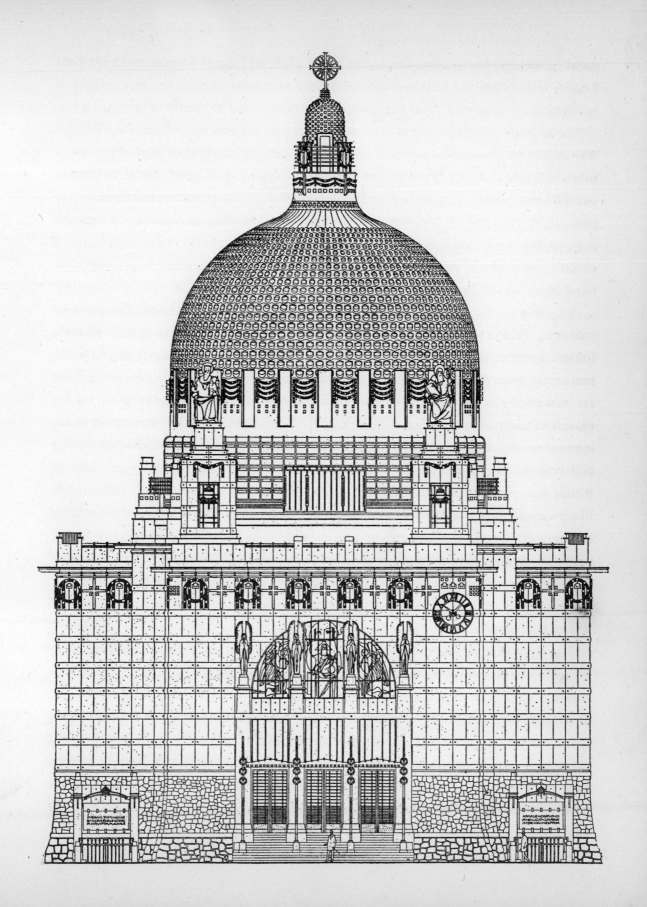

coffee-house world of letters into a new form at art, and the courageous editor of the *Fackel*, Karl Kraus.

When Hans Makart organized the great procession on 27 April 1879 to celebrate the silver wedding of the imperial couple, he himself dressed up as Peter Paul Rubens complete with plumed hat and dagger and the architectural designs were the work of Otto Wagner. Born in Penzing near Vienna in 1841, Otto Wagner began as a traditionalist but before long he had thrown overboard all the superfluous ballast of the past to become one of the foremost exponents of modern architecture. Hermann Bahr called him a 'mighty man, who lived and worked quietly, independent of all cliques, and who started a revolution', while Josef Hoffmann spoke of his 'genius for organizing on the grand scale'.

Wagner's public buildings changed the face of Vienna but without changing its character. The municipal railway stations and the sluice-building on the Danube Canal have a utilitarian simplicity, while elsewhere new but discreet forms of ornamentation were devised: in the court pavilion of the station at Schönbrunn the need for something more decorative was satisfied with rococo-like exuberance. In the design of the mental hospital at Steinhof, the dominating feature – the richly ornamented dome of the church – is an outstanding example of the Jugendstil or Art Nouveau and on the Linke Wienzeile he built two tenement-blocks, the walls of which are covered with delicate floral designs and light up the drab Mariahilferstadt like pages from a picture-book by Walter Crane. In the Post Office Savings Bank building, the severity of the cubist style is relieved by the closely-woven pattern on the flat façade and by the statues surrounding it; the War Ministry building, designed by Wagner, on the other side of the Stubenring would have provided an impressive companion-piece but in the end the baroque splendour of the Rudolf Baumann design was chosen.

Wagner's new architectural style inspired other outstanding artistic personalities. Joseph Olbrich, with the collaboration of the painter Klimt, designed the Secession building with its combination of cubes and curves, and Adolf Loos designed a commercial building on the Michaelerplatz which was the prototype of the new style, uncompromising in its lack of ornamentation and yet imaginative enough to avoid dullness. Because of his preference for ornamentation, Josef Hoffmann became known as 'Square Hoffmann'; unfortunately his masterpiece, the Palais Stocklet, is not in Vienna but in Brussels.

The first exhibition in the Secession building in 1898 set out not just to contrast the new generation with the old or one style with another but rather to encourage the artist *per se* as against the 'pedlar who pretends to be an artist'. The organizers were impressed by the pioneering work of William Morris, by the use made in America of contemporary materials, by Bing's Art Nouveau in Paris, by van de Velde and others like him in Hamburg, Berlin, Dresden and Munich. The desire to bring artists and craftsmen together in Vienna in a similar way led to the foundation of the 'Wiener Werkstätte' in 1903 by Josef Hoffmann, Kolo Moser and H. D. Czeschka.

Although the Viennese were perhaps the last to join the Arts and Crafts Movement in Europe, their contribution was all the more substantial and convincing, for the Viennese charm had at last found a new form of expression.

The Viennese opera also took on a new lease of life. Since 1875 the Hungarian Hans Richter, who had previously played the French horn in the orchestra at the Kärntnertor opera house, had been conducting in the splendid new building on the Ring; no conductor has ever flung himself with such untiring enthusiasm into the works of Richard Wagner. But it was not until Gustav Mahler arrived from Hamburg in 1897, first as conductor then as director, that the Opera acquired the tremendous artistic vitality that Schreyvogel, Laube and Burckhard had already injected into the Burgtheater.

Anna Bahr-Mildenburg speaks of Mahler's 'wonderful mixture of genius and pedantry' but she also mentions how difficult it was for him to admit when he was in the wrong. Mahler's repertoire looks rather conventional to the modern eye, consisting as it did of such novelties as Leoncavallo, Puccini, Tchaikowsky, Thuille and so on. After he had presented Richard Strauss's 'Feuersnot', he did, it is true, hope to produce 'Salome', but to his annoyance the censor refused permission. What was revolutionary was Mahler's style of production, in which he succeeded in giving a faithful rendering of the original work while at the same time reflecting his own period. And, to provide the appropriate décor, he brought in the brilliant exponent of the Secession Alfred Roller, of whom Anna Bahr-Mildenburg wrote: 'How beautiful and how overpowering everything was that Roller gave us and how closely it all matched Mahler's greatness!' They blew the dust off 'Don Juan' to give it new brilliance and their production of 'Tristan' opened up fresh vistas of Wagnerian interpretation.

In the concert field there was the same conflict between the traditional and the

ook illustration
y Kolo Moser in
er Sacrum, 1898

modern – and the ultra-modern. Apart from the symphonic poems of Strauss and the symphonies of Mahler, the first products of the New Viennese School also appeared: with a tremendous acoustic display Franz Schreker performed the post-Wagnerian, expressionist 'Gurrelieder' of Schönberg, who however had even more ambitious ideas and went on to evolve the so-called twelve-tone technique, after Matthias Hauer had developed his own twelve-tone theory in Vienna. Alban Berg combined the atonal system of his master Schönberg with his own, essentially Viennese musical fantasy, and Anton von Webern attained an unprecedented level of artistic perfection by paring away every superfluous note from his delicate compositions. At the same time in the great Opera House, Strauss's 'Frau ohne Schatten', produced in collaboration with Hofmannsthal and Roller, represented yet another Viennese fairy-tale with everything an orchestra had to offer.

Although the shy, polite Webern was so far ahead of his time as a composer, he continued to devote a great deal of time to his working men's choir and he particularly enjoyed conducting the popular Strauss waltzes. Oskar Nedbal, formerly, as viola-player, the heart and soul of the Bohemian String Quartet and later a successful composer of operettas, subsequently founded and directed a symphony orchestra and became a determined exponent of Mahler's music, while that famous moralist Karl Kraus was enthusing over the plays of Nestroy. In this same Vienna lived Franz Schmidt, composer of the opera 'Notre Dame' and such young and promising talents as Korngold, Wellesz and Křenek. Among the writers one young man called Loris was making a name for himself and only gradually did he come to put his real name to his essays and verse: Hugo von Hofmannsthal. Other prominent figures in the overlapping cultural circles of Vienna were the writer-librarian, officer and civil servant Robert Musil, the doctor-dramatists Schnitzler (who captured better than anyone else the fin-de-siècle atmosphere of Vienna) and Schönherr, the Zionists Theodor Herzl and Martin Buber, and from time to time Franz Kafka, Georg Trakl and Rainer Maria Rilke.

Even the gathering clouds of war did not dim the intellectual brilliance or even the vitality of the Viennese. For decades people had been living quite comfortably under the shadow of facile prophecies that Austria's end was near, and while the augurs kept their noses glued to foreign newspapers, the second generation of Viennese operetta celebrated one triumph after another. When the shots fired at Sarajevo finally unleashed the storm, there was a veritable mass flight into waltzing euphoria. The year

XII The Amusement Park in the Prater with its well-known landmark, the Giant Wheel

XIII The Kärntnerstrasse at night. This, the most famous thoroughfare in Vienna, is noted for its smart shops

Book illustration by Gustav Klimt in *Ver Sacrum*, 1898

1916 saw a record number of first performances with an operetta by Benatzky, three by Eysler, one by Fall, two by Jarno, one by Lehár, two by Nedbal, three by Stolz, one by Oscar Strauss and, the biggest success of all, Berte's 'Dreimäderlhaus' with music by Schubert; in the Court Opera House the second version of 'Ariadne auf Naxos' began its much more gradual climb to international fame.

On 12 November 1918 the Social Democrat leader Dr Karl Renner proclaimed the establishment of the Democratic Republic of German Austria, and the following year Vienna was confronted with a new and stark reality at Saint Germain: the non-German peoples had shaken themselves free but the union with Germany, which so many German Austrians hoped for, remained unfulfilled, and the proud imperial city had to make do as capital of a small State. The Social Democrats, who emerged from the first really free elections with a clear majority in Vienna itself, were at variance with the Christian Socialist Federal Government, which was predominantly clerical in its policy, and in July 1927, when the Palace of Justice went up in flames during public demonstrations, Austria hovered on the brink of civil war. Hitler's advent to power in Berlin gave a new lease of life to the idea of union, which had never been far from people's minds, the National Socialist movement in Austria gained ground rapidly, while the ruling clerical party tried to stem the flood that was rising both internally and externally with its own corporate state and the Patriotic Front.

Long before 1938 the cultural front in Vienna which had been built up during the Secession period and in which Jews had played such a prominent role, had crumbled. Kafka, Hofmannsthal, Schnitzler, Otto Stoessl, Alban Berg and Karl Kraus were all dead, Schönberg had moved to Berlin and from there to America, and Erich Wolfgang Korngold, in whom so many hopes had been placed, had also gone to America, while Kokoschka left for Prague in 1934 and eventually moved on to England; another who chose England was Felix Braun, Hofmannsthal's companion; Joseph Roth, author of the novel *Radetzkymarsch*, returned to Vienna from Berlin in 1933, only to flee again almost immediately. But the great exodus only began when Vienna became a sea of swastika banners and prepared herself to receive the German Führer and Chancellor. Max Reinhardt's last European assignment at the Josefstadt Theatre came to an abrupt end, the dramatist Ödön von Horváth, who had arrived from Germany in 1934, moved on to Paris; among the many who emigrated were Sigmund Freud, the musicians Wellesz and Křenek, the writers Werfel and Musil, Beer-Hoffmann and Salten, the music and drama critics Max Graf, Paul Stefan and Alfred

Polgar, the music publishers Erwin Stein and Ernst Roth. The highly versatile Egon Friedell, who at one time ran the controversial cabaret 'Fledermaus', took his own life when Hitler moved in.

Shortly afterwards came the humiliation of Prague, then the outbreak of war. The bombing of European cities spread to Vienna: incendiary bombs pierced the roof of St Stephen's Cathedral, destroyed the stage of the Opera House and struck the Burgtheater. When the Russian occupation began, it was as if a hurricane had hit the bewildered city, but, when the foreign troops had been there for ten years and the dust had settled, the Second Republic was firmly established, old differences had been smoothed out, the shadow-boxing had stopped and the need for collaboration had produced a new sense of realism. The war-damage was repaired, the federal theatres had returned to their new homes, and the vaulting of the Cathedral had been restored.

In the periods following the First and Second World Wars, when soldiers returned home to play their part in the cultural life of Vienna, new names appeared, amongst them the poets Alexander Lernet-Holenia and Heimito von Doderer; Franz Theodor Csokor and Franz Braun came back from their self-imposed exile, and if Oskar Kokoschka, who had retained his youthfulness longer than any of his contemporaries, remained abroad, he did not sever his links with Vienna.

The Republic was – and still is – no less active in its support of music and drama than the Imperial Court before it, and the Opera House on the Ring, the Burgtheater and all the other theatres with their wealth of local tradition, to say nothing of the Philharmonic and the Society of Friends of Music – all have continued to attract artists from every corner of the world. So it was inevitable that, despite the glamour of Salzburg, Vienna should also stake her claim to a place in the annual round of international summer festivals.

We must pause here, for we are approaching the present day when differences over artistic and administrative precedence are as rife as ever they were in the past, when the theatre still has its crises and no true Viennese can fail to take sides in the tug-of-war over trends and temperaments, over titles and honours. So I prefer not to trouble the reader with any further names but to leave him to make his own choice and apply his own censorship. But I think I owe it to him to indicate briefly the way in which the face of the city has changed in the republican period.

Vienna's population remained static for a long time after 1918. At the same time there was a powerful movement in the republic for social progress which, in competition with private enterprise, wrought far-reaching changes in the city.

Within the compass of the Ring the ancient buildings with their strong historical and artistic associations have been hard put to it to survive the claims of their commercial rivals that valuable sites would be better employed for buildings that grow taller and more profitable as time goes on. It was only beyond the 'Gürtel', which was once Vienna's outer line of defence, that the modern planner had freedom to operate. The first of these communal tenement-blocks, for example the Metzleinstaler Hof in the 5th District, the George Washington Hof in the 10th, the Karl Marx Hof in the 19th with its appropriate red walls, and the Karl Seitz Hof in the 21st, were built between the wars. As early as 1912 Josef Hoffmann's houses on the Kaasgrabengasse in the 19th District had created a new style in private dwellings; later Adolf Loos's housing-estate on the Heuberg and the 'Werkbund' estate built for the International Exhibition in 1929 were also pointers for the future. In the 'fifties there was a tremendous increase in building activities and today the suburbs of Vienna are full of tenement buildings, of varying aesthetic standards, which were constructed with the help of the Municipality. And a new feature of Vienna's skyline are the multi-storey buildings of the insurance companies and other financial concerns, particularly along the Danube Canal; sports grounds, an attractive Town Hall, pedestrian subways elegantly laid out under the main traffic-crossings on the Ring, the West and South railway-stations and the inviting reception building of the airport at Schwechat, all combine to present an image of Vienna in the second half of the twentieth century. And motor-cars wherever one goes or stands. . . .

But I would like to invite the reader to make his way back into the alleyways down which Beethoven walked, into a 'Beisl' or two where Nestroy drank his tankard of beer, into one of the surviving coffee-houses where in Altenberg's day one was still served with a 'Wolkenbruch' ('cloudburst') consisting of six glasses of water, to the palace where Maria Theresa listened to young Mozart, to the rooms where Prince Eugene once pored over his books and engravings, and to the auditorium of the theatre where even the most enterprising of producers cannot destroy the magic of a work by Grillparzer, Raimund, Gluck, or the immortal 'Fledermaus'.

THE PLATES

1–8 *St Stephen's Cathedral*, consecrated in 1147 as parish church of the see of Passau, 1365 diocesan church, 1469–79 seat of the newly-created Bishopric of Vienna, since 1732 Metropolitan Cathedral of the Archbishop. The original Romanesque building was replaced in the thirteenth century by a building in the late Romanesque style, of which the west façade with the 'Riesentor' still survives (ill. 2). In 1304–40 the early Gothic 'Albertine' halled choir was built. The Gothic 'Rudolfian' nave was started in 1359 and the vault was completed around 1450 by the cathedral architect Hans Puchspaum. The south tower, which soars up in the centre of the city and has become the symbol of Vienna (1 and colour plate I, page 9), was started in the middle of the fourteenth century and completed in 1439.

3 In the Gothic period there was a pointed arch in front of the 'Riesentor'; on the inside of what was the base of the arch is a figure which, it is assumed, represents the Works Superintendent who controlled the finances, while opposite him was another figure, presumably that of the Master Builder.

4, 5 The pulpit, which was built 1514/15, is the main work of the architect Anton Pilgram. The four priestly figures on the front represent the four human temperaments. Pilgram produced two effigies of himself, one at the base of the pulpit (4), where he is seen looking out of a window, the other as a console supporting the organ in the north wall of the nave (colour plate II, page 19).

6–8 Each of the great pillars between the nave and the aisles has three life-size figures from the fifteenth century.

9 View down the Salvatorgasse of the tower of the *Maria am Gestade* or Maria Stiegen Church, which dates back to the eleventh century and was restored several times. The tower was built 1394–1414 by the ducal architect Michael Knab, was damaged in the first Turkish siege and restored 1534–37.

10 The *Church of St Rupert* was considered the oldest church in Vienna as early as the thirteenth century. The present Romanesque building dates back to the twelfth century.

11 *St Michael's Church*, formerly the imperial parish church of St Michael, replaced an earlier building in the thirteenth century. In the Gothic choir at the end of the Romanesque nave one can see the richly-decorated high altar of Jean B. d'Avrange, 1781. Ill. 128 shows the neo-classical façade with Matielli's group of angels.

12 On the southern approach-road, today the Triesterstrasse, where public executions were carried out until 1868, the cathedral architect Hans Puchspaum built the '*Spinnerin am Kreuz*' (Woman Spinning at the Cross) in 1451–52, replacing an older statue.

13 The former *Church of the Minors,* now the Italian National Church of Maria Schnee. The west doorway of the new Gothic building with its sculptures dates back to around 1350. The figure on the right of the crucifixion group in the tympanum is the founder, Duke Albrecht II.

1 ST. STEPHAN

3

4

2-5 ST. STEPHAN

2

6-8
ST. STEPHAN

7

8

9 MARIA AM GESTADE
10 ST. RUPRECHT
11 ST. MICHAEL
12 SPINNERIN AM KREUZ

11

12

14 The *Church of St Charles* (see also colour plate VI, page 59) was built to commemorate St Carlo Borromeo as the result of a vow taken by Emperor Charles VI during the plague of 1713. Johann Bernhard Fischer von Erlach's design was chosen in competition with Ferdinando Galli-Bibiena and Johann Lucas von Hildebrandt. In 1724–39 Joseph Emmanuel Fischer von Erlach carried on the work which his father had started in 1716–22, and made certain alterations in the original design. The dome was built in 1725. The side view shows that the dome, which appears circular in the familiar front view, is in fact oval-shaped.

15 The *Salvator Chapel* by the Town Hall, originally private chapel of the von Neuburg family, today church of the 'Old Catholics', was adorned with its elaborate Renaissance doorway in 1513–30. The originals of the two figures of knights are now in the Historical Museum, having been replaced by copies.

16 The '*Stock im Eisen*' in the old horse market, today at the corner of the Kärntnerstrasse and the Graben, is a tree-trunk encircled by an iron band and thickly studded with nails. It is a popular feature of old Vienna, which is alleged to have been part of a forest that reached this point and which was preserved when the building that stood here previously was demolished.

17 View down the Rotenturmstrasse towards the upper meat market and showing the back of the '*Kornhäuselturm*' next to St Rupert's Church, built by the architect Josef Kornhäusel 1825–27 and inhabited by Adalbert Stifter 1842–48.

18 Renaissance courtyard of the sixteenth century '*Bürgerhaus*' at No. 7 Bäckerstrasse.

19 *St Peter's Church* (see also colour plate VIII, page 79), the collegiate and municipal parish church of St Peter, is reputed to have been founded by Charlemagne. The present baroque building was started in 1702 by Gabriele Montani and after 1703 Johann Lucas von Hildebrandt presumably took over; the main structure was completed in 1708. The façade, which dates back to 1722, was completed between 1751 and 1753 with the addition of a projecting porch with sculptures in lead by Franz Kohl. The splendid interior is dominated by the oval-shaped dome; the stucco-work was by Albert Camesina, while Santino Bussi decorated the choir, Antonio Galli-Bibiena designed the high altar and Matthias Steinl the chancel.

20 The *Church of the Piarists*, the parish church of 'Maria Treu' in Josefstadt, was started some time after 1716 and the design is attributed to Hildebrandt. In 1771 it was finally consecrated. Behind the main dome is a second over the altar, both with painted ceilings by Franz Anton Maulpertsch. The chancel was the work of Johann Josef Rössler, the altar-piece of Karl Rahl.

21 The *Schottenkirche* (Church of the Scots) on the Freyung, abbey and parish church (of Our Lady), was originally part of a monastery founded in 1155 by the Babenberg Duke Heinrich

II 'Jasomirgott'. The building was restored several times, the last two occasions being in the nineteenth century and after the bombing raids of 1945. The magnificent baroque interior was the work of Andrea Allio and Silvestro Carlone, the high altar was added by Heinrich von Ferstel in 1883.

22 The *Church of St Charles* (see note on ill. 14): the angel on the right of the main porch, also the companion figure, by Franz Caspar, behind it one of the two victory columns modelled on Trajan's Column in Rome and decorated with spiral reliefs which depict scenes from the life of St Carlo Borromeo, by J. B. Mader, J. B. Straub and J. Schlitterer, 1728–30.

23 *Jesuit Church of the Nine Angelic Choirs*: this Carmelite church, which was built around 1400, was transferred to the Jesuits in 1553 and Carlo A. Carlone was responsible for its façade, an outstanding example of early Viennese baroque. From its balcony Pope Pius VI blessed the Viennese on the occasion of his visit to Joseph II in 1782 and in 1806 heralds announced the end of the Holy Roman Empire.
On the 'Am Hof' Square in front of the church stands the *Column of Our Lady*, built in 1644 by the Emperor Ferdinand III in thanksgiving for the preservation of Vienna from the Swedes. Modelled on the marble Column of Our Lady in Munich, it was moved to Wernstein Castle in 1667 and replaced by a new column in bronze by B. Herold on a marble base by C. M. Carlone and C. Canevale.

24 The *Church of the Jesuits*, the University Church of the Assumption which dates from 1628–31 when the University was rebuilt following a bequest by Emperor Ferdinand III. It was given its present magnificent interior in 1703–07 by the architect and sculptor Andrea Pozzo, a master of the sumptuous baroque religious style.

25 The *Church of the Augustinians*, the court parish church built in the fourteenth century, where imperial church ceremonies were usually held, including the funeral services for the emperors. This outstanding tomb is one of the main works of Antonio Canova, who built it between 1798 and 1805 for the Archduchess Maria Christine, Maria Theresa's favourite daughter, who married Duke Albrecht of Sachsen-Teschen.

15 SALVATORKAPELLE

16 STOCK IM EISEN

17 KORNHÄUSELTURM

18 BÄCKERSTRASSE 7

19 ST. PETER   20 PIARISTENKIRCHE

21 SCHOTTENKIRCHE

22 KARLSKIRCHE

23

24

25 AUGUSTINERKICHE. GRABMAL ERZHERZOGIN MARIA CHRISTINE

26–37, 113 The Imperial Palace dates back to the thirteenth century; the earliest known pictures dating
from the late fifteenth century show the 'Schweizertrakt' or Swiss wing of Rudolf von
Habsburg with the chapel built 1447–49 by Emperor Frederick III. Among the additions
during the Renaissance period was the *Swiss Gate* (colour plate III, p. 29) which led into the
'Swiss Courtyard'. According to an inscription dated 1552 it was built on the instructions of
Emperor Ferdinand I, presumably by the imperial architect, Pietro Ferrabosco.

26 The southern approach to the citadel, the *Outer Gate*, replaced the former gate in the city
walls. It was started in 1818 following a competition which was won by Luigi Cagnola and
was completed in 1824 by Peter von Nobile. Rudolf Wondra transformed the interior into a
heroes' memorial in 1933–34.

27 In the middle of the *Josefsplatz* stands the *equestrian statue of Emperor Joseph II*, the work of
Franz Anton Zauner between 1795 and 1807. Behind it is the right wing of the library building, constructed by Nikolaus Pacassi in 1763–69, with the windows of the great Redoutensaal,
scene of many famous social and musical occasions.

28 The east front of the *Imperial Library*, today the National Library, on the Josefsplatz was
designed by Johann Bernhard Fischer von Erlach and built by his son Joseph Emanuel in
1723–35; the sculptures on the dome-like mansard-roof were the work of Lorenzo Matielli
and Hans Gasser.

29 The splendid *Gallery of the Imperial Library*, is one of the finest interiors of the late baroque
period with a painted ceiling by Daniel Gran. On the bookshelves is Prince Eugene's library
with its precious leather bindings, which the Emperor acquired after the Prince's death. In
the middle of the room stands a marble statue of Charles VI by Strudel.

30 The *Winter Riding School* (photo H. Kopezki), built by Joseph Emanuel Fischer von Erlach
between 1729 and 1735 on the site of the old 'Paradeisgartl', was the largest room in the
Imperial Palace and was frequently the scene of brilliant official functions, particularly during
the Congress of Vienna. It houses the Spanish Riding School and the *haute école* performances
by the white Lipizza stallions were a traditional feature of the Imperial Court which has been
perpetuated to this day. The Lipizza stallions are a cross-breed of Andalusian, Arab and
Neapolitan horses, and the strain was started in 1580 by Archduke Charles, son of Ferdinand
I, on his stud-farm at Lipizza in Carniole. The Lipizzans proved outstanding not only in
battle but also in the equine ballets, which Leopold I was particularly fond of, and they
were also used to draw the Emperor Francis Joseph's state-coach. Under the Republic the
stud-farm was moved to Piber, near Köflach, in Styria. The Lipizzans, which have become
state property, are housed in the Stallburg (31) in Vienna.

31 The courtyard of the *Stallburg*, which was built 1558–65, still shows traces of the old Renaissance imperial palace.

32 A Lipizza stallion in the Spanish Riding School. (Photo H. Kopezki.)

33 In the *Inner Courtyard* of the Palace stands the statue of Emperor Francis I (as the last German Emperor: Francis II), which was the work of Pompeo Marchesi in 1842–46. On the north-west side is the Amelienburg with its belfry, on the north-east side the long façade of the Imperial Chancellery, designed by Joseph Emanuel Fischer.

34 The Michaelerplatz entrance to the *Inner Courtyard* of the Palace. The gateways in the Reichskanzleitrakt (see also engraving on page 51) are flanked by massive groups of statuary by Lorenzo Matielli, representing the labours of Hercules.

35 The *Michaelertrakt*: the monumental entrance to the Palace from the Michaelerplatz was originally designed by J. E. Fischer von Erlach but was not built until 1889–93 by Ferdinand Kirschner in the new baroque style.

36 Inside the passage leading from the Michaelertrakt to the Inner Courtyard a gate with appropriately decorated pediment was preserved from the *old Burgtheater*, which had to make way for the Michaelertrakt.

37 In the Palace Chapel there are regular performances by the Vienna boy singers. This traditional choir, to which Joseph Haydn and Franz Schubert formerly belonged, was founded by the Emperor Maximilian I. (Photo Lothar Rübelt.)

IVSTITIA. REGNORVM. FVNDAMENTVM.

26-37 HOFBURG

27 JOSEFSPLATZ

30, 32
WINTERREITSCH

31 STALLBURG

38 *Apotheosis of Prince Eugene.* Marble sculpture by Balthasar Permoser, dating from 1718–21, in the Baroque Museum of the Lower Belvedere.

39 Air photograph (by Landesbildstelle Wien-Burgenland) of the *Belvedere*, showing the Lower Belvedere at the foot of the picture, the Upper Belvedere at the top of the garden. The estate, which lies about three-quarters of a mile to the south of the city walls and rises gently southwards, was acquired by Prince Eugene in 1693 as a site for a summer residence. In 1700 the ground was terraced and between 1700 and 1725 the Gardens were designed by the Bavarian Director of Gardens, Dominique Girard, and laid out by the Inspector of Gardens, Anton Zinner. Johann Lucas von Hildebrandt was commissioned to plan the buildings and in 1714–16 completed the Lower Belvedere, which the Prince used as a summer residence. A number of outstanding decorators and painters were employed on the interior (see also ill. 74 with the Marble Hall, in which the original figures from the Providentia Fountain are displayed today). The Upper Belvedere was built 1721–22 and was used only for special receptions and festivities.
After the Prince's death, his heiress, Victoria of Savoy, Duchess of Sachsen-Hildburghausen sold the property to the Emperor. After the First World War the Lower Belvedere was turned into a Museum of Baroque Art, suffered bomb damage in 1945, was restored and reopened in 1953. In the Upper Belvedere Joseph II housed the imperial art gallery in 1777, which became the Art History Museum in 1890. In 1894 the heir to the throne, Franz Ferdinand, took up residence in the Upper Belvedere; today it houses the 'nineteenth and twentieth Century Gallery'. In the Marble Hall of the Upper Belvedere on 15 May 1955 the Austrian State Treaty was signed, which brought to an end the ten years of occupation by the Russian, British, French and American forces. (See also colour plate IV, p. 39), which shows the south gateway surmounted by the coat of arms of Savoy and the south façade of the Lower Belvedere with the glass front which was built on later.)

40 Garden fronting the *Lower Belvedere.*

41 The Entrance Hall of the *Upper Belvedere* contains four giant atlantes, which were not in the original design. An important part in the interior decoration of the palace was played by Claude Le Fort du Plessy and the stucco-artist Santino Bussi.

42 Main staircase in the *Upper Belvedere.*

43–47 The *Town Palace of Prince Eugene in the Himmelpfortgasse*, also known as the Winter Palace (see on pages 44–45 the engraving from the great architectural work by Fischer von Erlach), was designed by Fischer von Erlach the Elder in 1695–96. Work on the building began in 1697, in 1702 Johann Lucas von Hildebrandt took over and in 1708–09, after some of the neighbouring property had been purchased, he extended the building towards the Seilerstätte and in

1723–24 towards the Kärntnerstrasse. In 1704, when Prince Eugene returned from his victory, together with Marlborough, at Höchstädt (Blindheim), an imperial decree declared the palace to be a 'privileged free house, which for all time shall be free from any tax, billeting or any other burden'. The Prince died here on 21 April 1736 and the palace became imperial property. It was subsequently occupied by the Ministry of Mines and, from 1848 onwards, by the Ministry of Finance.

43, 46 The portals in the Himmelpfortgasse are decorated with relief sculptures of scenes from ancient mythology and history by Lorenzo Matielli: on the east portal Achilles can be seen riding over Hector's dead body (43); on the west portal, which was added later by Hildebrandt, the victorious general is presented as a bringer of peace (46).

44, 45 The staircase, which was designed by Johann Bernhard Fischer von Erlach, is dominated by four gigantic atlantes by the sculptor Giovanni Giuliani.

47 The reception rooms on the first floor show a marked French influence in the interior décor.

39-42 BELVEDERE

43   44

43-47 STADTPALAIS PRINZ EUGEN AN DER HIMMELPFORTGASSE

48–50   The *Palais Kinsky* was built for Count Philipp Daun in 1713–16 to Hildebrandt's design and was later acquired by Prince Kinsky. The beautifully symmetrical façade giving on to the Freyung (48) and the staircase (49, 50) with its niche-sculptures and the balustrade with its frolicsome cherubs are among the finest and best preserved works of Viennese Baroque. The ceiling above the staircase (colour plate V, page 49) was painted by Gaetano Fanti in the pseudo-architectural style and by Carlo Carlone (with the help of Chiarini) who depicted the glorification of a hero.

51   The former *Bohemian Imperial Chancellery*, now occupied by the Constitutional and Administrative Court, was built 1708–14 to a design by J. B. Fischer von Erlach and was later altered several times, but the façade on the Wipplingerstrasse has remained largely unchanged. The rich sculptural decoration round the entrance-doors was mostly the work of Lorenzo Matielli.

52   The former *Imperial Stables*, which are now used to house exhibitions, were conceived by J. B. Fischer von Erlach and constructed 1719–23 by his son Joseph Emanuel in a somewhat different form.

53   The building complex which had served as a *Town Hall* since the fourteenth century was given its fine baroque façade in the Wipplingerstrasse around 1700 in the style of J. B. Fischer von Erlach.

54   The *Palais Lobkowitz* was built 1685–87 to a design by Giovanni Pietro Tencala for Prince Dietrichstein; the doorway in this photograph was the work of J. B. Fischer von Erlach about 1710. In the Eroica Hall Prince Lobkowitz's orchestra gave first performances of Beethoven's compositions.

55   The present *Federal Chancellery*, seat of the Austrian Government on the Ballhausplatz, was built 1717–19 to a design by Hildebrandt to house the Imperial Privy Council and was subsequently extended. Princes Kaunitz and Metternich and other leading Austrian personalities had their official residence here.

56   The *Josephinum* on the Währingerstrasse was built 1783–85 by Isidor Canevale, to accommodate the Academy of Surgical Medicine. The work was commissioned by Joseph II.

57–58   The former *Palais Starhemberg* on the Minoritenplatz, residence of the defender of Vienna in 1683, is occupied today by the Ministry of Education. The building, which dates back to the sixteenth century, was restored in the seventeenth century; the classical staircase is adorned with sculptures by Joseph Kleiber.

59   The *Stadtpalais Liechtenstein* was begun in 1694 for Count Kaunitz to a design by Domenico

Martinelli and, after it had been acquired by Prince Liechtenstein, was completed in 1706 by Gabriel de Gabrieli. The ornate doorway on the Minoritenplatz belongs to the later period.

60–63 *Schönbrunn Palace*, built 1696–1713 by J. B. Fischer von Erlach on the site of a hunting-lodge as a summer-residence for Joseph I, was finally completed under Maria Theresa in 1744–49 by Nikolaus Pacassi and thereafter was the favourite residence of the imperial family. The Grand Gallery (62, photo Toni Schneider) has a painted ceiling by Gregorio Guglielmi, dating from 1760–62. The gardens (60, air photo Landesbildstelle Wien-Burgenland) were laid out in 1705–06 by Jean Trehet and redesigned under Maria Theresa by Jadot de Ville-Issey around 1750; further alterations were made after 1765 by Ferdinand Hohenberg, who built the Gloriette at the highest point in the gardens to commemorate the victory at Kolin. The Naiad Fountain (61) and its companion-piece were both designed by J. B. Hagenauer. The 'Roman Ruin' (63), which dates from 1778, is an example of the romantic taste for ruins prevalent at that time.

64 The *Landhaus*, seat of the Land Government of Lower Austria, formerly the Liechtenstein Freihaus, was taken over in 1513 by the Estates of Lower Austria and was extended in 1837–48, when the pillared façade was built. It was here that the first violent demonstrations took place in March 1848 and on 21 October 1918 the Republic of Austria came into being.

65 The former *Bürgerliche Zeughaus* (Armoury), today a fire-station, was built in the sixteenth century; its baroque façade by Anton Ospel, with figures by Matielli, was added in 1731–32.

66 The *Palais Pallavicini* on the Josefsplatz was built 1783–84 by Ferdinand von Hohenberg for the future Count Fries; the caryatid doorway was the work of Franz Anton Zauner.

67 The former *Hochholzerhof* on the Tuchlauben acquired its baroque façade in 1719.

68 The *Palais Schwarzenberg* on the Rennweg, built 1697–1704 to a design by Hildebrandt as a garden palace for Prince Mansfeld-Fondi, passed into the hands of Prince von Schwarzenberg in 1716, who commissioned both the Elder and the Younger Fischer von Erlach to extend the original buildings.

69–70 The former *Palais Rasumowsky*, which is occupied today by the Federal Institute of Geology, was built 1806–07 by Louis von Montoyer for the Russian ambassador, Count Rasumowsky, to whom Beethoven dedicated his 'Rasumowsky Quartet', op. 59. After a fire in 1814 and again after bomb-damage in 1945, it was restored. The neo-classical banqueting-hall, which is characteristic of the period of the Vienna Congress, was the scene of many soirées organized by the Count, who was a great lover of music.

71 The *Aula* (Great Hall) of the old University, today occupied by the Academy of Sciences, was built 1753–55 to a design by Jean Nicolas Jadet de Ville-Issey, commissioned by Maria Theresa. The statues in the mural foundations have been ascribed to Joseph Lenzbauer.

48-50
PALAIS KINSKY

54 PALAIS
   LOBKOWITZ

55 BUNDESKANZ
   AMT

56 JOSEPHINUM

55

56

57

58

57-58 PALAIS STARHEMBERG

59 PALAIS LIECHTENSTEIN

60

61

62

72 The *Andromeda Fountain* in one of the courtyard walls of the Old Town Hall was built in 1741 by Georg Raphael Donner, whom the City of Vienna commissioned. Under the balcony, which is supported by cherubs and surrounded by a balustrade wrought by Simon Vogl in 1725, is a lead relief which depicts Perseus fighting the monster, with Andromeda in the foreground.

73-74 The *Providentia Fountain* in the New Market, the former **Grain Market**, which is more commonly known as the *Donner Fountain*, is the outstanding work of Georg Raphael Donner, who was commissioned by the city authorities in favour of his distinguished competitor, Matielli. The originals of the lead figures, executed jointly with Johann Nikolaus Moll, were replaced by bronze copies in 1873 and are to be seen today in the Baroque Museum in the Marble Hall of the Lower Belvedere.
In the centre of the fountain the figure of Providentia, round the basin the rivers March personified as river-goddess (73), the Enns as a ferryman (74), the Traun and the Ybbs. Maria Theresa took exception to the naked figures and had them removed in 1770; the sculptor J. M. Fischer, who was instructed to melt them down, saw to it that they were preserved and they were restored to their former position in 1801.

75 View from the New Market with the *Providentia Fountain* in the foreground of the Plankengasse and the *Evangelical Church H.B.*, the Reformed Church which was built 1783–84 by Gottlieb Nigelli; the façade and the tower were rebuilt in 1887.

76 In the square in front of the *Franciscan Church* of St Jerome with its early seventeenth-century Renaissance façade stands the *Moses Fountain*. The lead statue and the reliefs representing the Jews in the desert were the work of Johann Martin Fischer in 1798. Prior to that the fountain itself was in the courtyard of the Haus zum grünen Löwen next door.

77 The *Mariä-Vermählungs-Brunnen* (Mary's Wedding Fountain) in the High Market, also known as the Joseph Column, was erected as a result of a vow by Leopold I to dedicate a monument to St Joseph if the heir to the throne, Joseph (I), returned safely from the siege of Landau during the war of the Spanish Succession. J. B. Fischer von Erlach erected a wooden pillar in 1706 on the spot where gallows and a pillory had stood. Then in 1729–32 his son Joseph Emanuel created the present monument in marble with a bronze baldachin supported by pillars. The marble group with Mary, Joseph and the High Priest was the work of Antonio Corradini.

78-79 The *Plague Column* on the Graben, dedicated to the Holy Trinity and the Nine Angelic Choirs owes its existence to a vow taken by the Emperor Leopold I during the Great Plague of 1679. The first column, which was in wood, by Joseph Frühwirt, was replaced 1682–93 by the present, much more elaborate column in stone. The basic plan was by Dr Franz Menegatti, the design by Mathias Rauchmiller, but the court architect Lodovico Ottavio Burnacini seems to have been largely responsible for the work as a whole in collaboration with a number of other artists, among them the young Johann Bernhard Fischer (von Erlach), who was involved in designing the base of the column. The group with the Emperor Leopold I kneeling (79) and the angel above is by Paul Strudel, the bronze group of the Trinity at the top of the column by Johann Kilian.

80 In front of the choir of the *Ulrichs Church* of Maria Trost in the 7th District, which was restored in the eighteenth century, stands a *Plague Column* dating back to 1713. This column simulating clouds is crowned by statues representing the Holy Trinity; on the base are statues representing the Virgin Mary and St Roch.

81 On the north side of the choir of St Stephen is the *Capistran Pulpit*, built around 1430 and named after Johannes Capistranus, who is reputed to have delivered fiery sermons on this spot in 1451, calling on the faithful to join a crusade against the Turks. In 1737 the baroque superstructure was added, with the figure of the famous preacher, who was canonized in 1690. Design by Franz von Roettiers, sculptures by Johann Josef Rössler.

ROMEDA-
BRUNNEN

74

DIVO·IOSEPHO·E·DAVIDICA·STIRPE
DEIPARAE·VIRGINIS·VIRO
CHRISTI·SERVATORIS·NUTRITIO
PRAESENTISSIMO·AUSTRIAE·PATRONO
NUNCUPATUM·LEOPOLDO·&·IOSEPHO·AUGG·
VOTUM
CAROLUS·VI·ROM·IMP·ET·HISPAN·REX
A·PATRE·AC·FRATRE·ADUMBRATUM·OPUS
AERE·AC·MARMORE·DE·INTEGRO·EXSTRUENS
M·L·

LEOPOLD I.

82 Maria Theresa in Hungarian coronation regalia. Lead figure by Franz Xaver Messerschmidt in the Baroque Museum in the Lower Belvedere.

83–84 Under the Church of the Capuchins on the New Market lies the *Imperial Vault*, in which almost all members of the ruling house since 1633 are buried. The most impressive monument is the double sarcophagus of pewter which was made for Maria Theresa and her husband Francis I by Balthasar Ferdinand Moll in 1753, while the imperial couple were still alive (Francis I died in 1765, the Empress in 1780). At the corners of the sarcophagus four mourning figures hold the crowns of the four realms of the empire; on its lid are life-size effigies of the imperial couple.

85 The *Mozart Memorial* was designed by Viktor Tilger in 1896 and erected in the Albertinaplatz; after the Second World War it was moved to its present position in the palace garden.

86 *Joseph Haydn* spent the twelve years prior to his death on 31 May 1809 in this house in the Haydngasse in the Mariahilfe (6th) District.

87 In the *Figarohaus* between the Schulerstrasse and the Domgasse Mozart lived from 1784 to 1787, during which time he composed, *inter alia,* his opera 'The Marriage of Figaro'.

88 The *Augarten,* first laid out in the seventeenth century and redesigned in 1712, was opened to the public by Joseph II in 1755; over the entrance-gate, built by Isidor Canevale, the Emperor had his own personal dedication inscribed.

89 The parkland of the *Prater,* which had been a game-preserve since the time of the Emperor Maximilian II, was opened to the public by Joseph II in 1766. The *Lusthaus* at the eastern end of the main avenue was rebuilt to its present design in 1782 by Isidor Canevale.

90 Above the *Papageno Door* of the *Theater an der Wien,* which was reconstructed several times and where Mozart's 'The Magic Flute', Beethoven's 'Fidelio' and many other works were first performed, the group representing Papageno and his children, dates from around 1800.

91 Mozart and Albrechtsberger, who taught Beethoven the theory of music, were among those who played the organ of the parish church of *St Lawrence* in the Schottenfeld.

92–94 Among the many houses in or around Vienna where Beethoven is known to have lived for longer or shorter period the following are still standing: the *Pasqualische Haus* on the Mölker Bastei 8 (92) where Beethoven lived on several occasions from 1804 onwards, the Rokokohaus in the Kahlenbergstrasse in *Nussdorf* (93), where he spent the summers of 1817 and 1824, *No. 5 Ungargasse* (94), where the Ninth Symphony was completed in 1823–24; *No. 8 Grinzingerstrasse* between Grinzing and Heiligenstadt (colour plate VII, page 69), where Beethoven and the Grillparzer family lived together; and the seventeenth-century house on the Pfauplatz in *Heiligenstadt* (153), where Beethoven spent some weeks in 1817.

95 The *Beethoven Memorial* of 1800 in the Beethovenplatz is one of the outstanding works of the sculptor Kaspar Zumbusch.

96 Johann Strauss the Younger lived in this house, No. 18 Maxingstrasse between 1870 and 1878, when he composed, *inter alia,* 'Die Fledermaus'.

97 *Johann Strauss the Elder*: Medallion on his tomb in the Central Cemetery.

98 Dancing couple on the *Monument for Johann Strauss the Elder and Josef Lanner* in the Rathaus-park, designed by Seifert and Örly in 1905.

99–100 Portraits of the singers *Josephine Gallmeyer* (1838–84) and *Marie Geistinger* (1836–1903) on their tombstones in the Central Cemetery.

101 The *Memorial to Johann Strauss the Younger* by Edmund Hellmer, which has been in the Municipal Park since 1923, takes the form of a bronze statue of the composer, playing the violin, under a marble arch decorated with relief carvings.

102 The house at No. 54 Nussdorferstrasse (9th District), where *Franz Schubert* was born on 31 January 1797, is a typical two-storey suburban house of the period.

103 The Kustodentrakt of the Upper Belvedere, where *Anton Bruckner* died on 11 October 1896.

104 The *Theater in der Josefstadt* was altered in 1822 by Joseph Kornhäusel and restored in 1841. A medallion above the entrance with a head of Max Reinhardt, whose last creative years in Europe were spent here, is a reminder of one of the most brilliant periods in the history of this former suburban theatre.

105 *Memorial to Ferdinand Raimund* by Franz Vogel, 1898, in the Weghuberpark near the Volks-theater.

106 In the former *Währinger Ortsfriedhof*, which became the Schubertpark in 1925, Beethoven and Schubert (who today lie in the Central Cemetery) and Grillparzer (now in the Hietzinger Cemetery) were originally buried. An eighteenth-century baroque cross stands in the part of the cemetery which has been preserved.

107–108 In the 'St-Marxer' Cemetery with its tombstones from the Biedermeier period is a tombstone from 1859 on the spot where Mozart was once buried.

109–110 The cenotaphs of *Johannes Brahms* and *Hugo Wolf* (the latter by Edmund Hellmer, 1904) in the Central Cemetery.

111 The *Grillparzer Memorial* was erected in 1889 in the Volksgarten, architecture by Hasenauer, statue by Karl Kundmann.

112 The house at No. 12 Salesianergasse in which *Hugo von Hofmannsthal* was born on 1 February 1874.

84

83-84 SARKOPHAG FRANZ I. / MARIA THERESIA

86

85 MOZART-DENKMAL

86 HAYDN-HAUS
87 FIGARO-HAUS

87

88

89

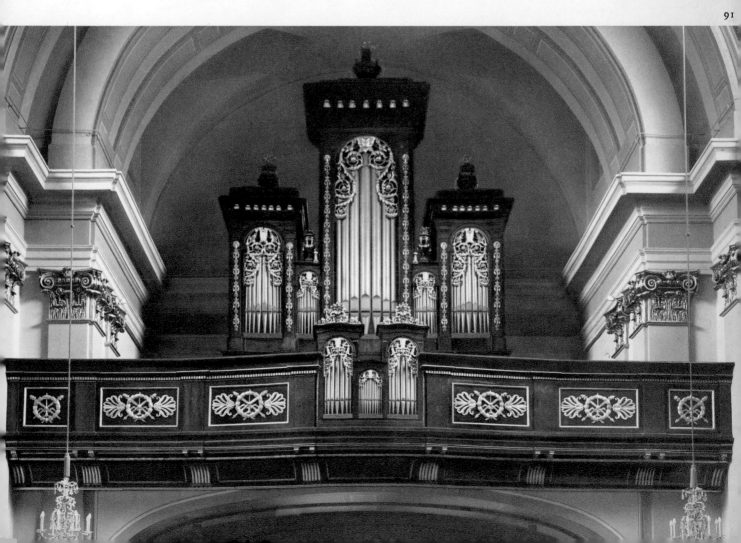

92

93

94

LUDWIG

VAN

96

97

98

99

100

104

105

106

HUGO·WOLF
MDCCCLX·MCMIII

BRAHMS

1833 - 1897

106 WÄHRINGER FRIEDHOF
107-108 ST.-MARXER FRIEDHOF
109-110 ZENTRALFRIEDHOF

III GRILLPARZER-DENKMAL
II2 HOFMANNSTHAL-GEBURTSHAUS

113 The *Neue Hofburg* (New Imperial Palace) was started in 1881 by Carl Hasenauer and only completed in 1913 by Friedrich Ohmann. It was intended as the centre-piece of an imperial forum, designed by Gottfried Semper and only partially completed. The façade forms a grandiose background to the equestrian statue of Prince Eugene, which Anton Fernkorn created in 1853–59.

114 The *Kunsthistorische Museum* was to form part, together with the National History Museum opposite, of Semper's imperial forum. This building with its Renaissance façade designed by Semper was built between 1871 and 1891 by Carl Hasenauer to accommodate the imperial collection of paintings. Between the two museums on Maria Theresa Square stands the Maria Theresa monument, completed in 1887, architecture by Hasenauer, the bronze figures of the Empress and the statesmen and generals around her by Kaspar Zumbusch.

115 The *Parliament Building*, built 1873–83 to a design by the Dane Theophil Hansen as the seat of the Imperial Council, is outstanding among the buildings on the Ring as a monumental example of the classical style with Athene fountain and groups of horses in front of the temple-like façade.

116 The *Theseus Temple* in the *Volksgarten*, a copy made by Peter Nobile, in 1820–23, of the Theseion in Athens, was originally built to accommodate the Theseus group of Canova, which is in the Art History Museum. In the background, the Gothic façade of the Rathaus, built by Friedrich von Schmid in 1872–83.

117 The *Votivkirche*, the diocesan Church of the Saviour, was built to commemorate the unsuccessful attempt to assassinate the young Emperor in 1853. In open competition the design chosen was by the twenty-seven-year-old Heinrich Ferstel, who was inspired by the Gothic cathedrals of France. The church was built 1856–79.

118 The *Austria Fountain* on the Freyung is a typical product of the Munich romantic school. It was created by Ludwig Schwanthaler in 1844–46. Under the figure of Austria are the rivers Danube, Po, Elbe and Vistula.

119 The main building of the *University* on the Dr Karl-Lueger-Ring was built 1873–83 to a design by Heinrich Ferstel, architect of the Votivkirche, who drew his inspiration in this case from the Renaissance.

120 The *Albertina*, where the valuable 'Albertina' graphic art collection of the Austrian National Library is housed, was originally the eighteenth-century Palais Taroucca reconstructed by Louis von Montoyer in 1801–04. The façade was altered in 1867 and, following bomb-damage in 1945, was rebuilt, leaving out some of the plastic decoration. In the surrounding wall is

the Neo-Baroque *Danubius Fountain* of 1869, architecture by Moritz von Loehr, marble statues by Johann Meixner, above it the equestrian statue of the Archduke Albrecht by Karl Zumbusch, 1899.

121 The construction of the new *Opera House*, formerly the Court Opera, now the State Opera, was the first large building to appear in the newly-opened Ring and the contract was awarded, after an open competition, to the architects Eduard van der Nüll and August Siccardsburg. On 25 May 1869 the opening ceremony took place. Following severe bomb-damage in 1945, work of restoration was carried out by Erich Boltenstern, who completed it in 1955; the exterior remained unchanged but the interior was entirely redesigned. (See also illustrations 118 and 120.)

122 *The Evangelical Church A.B.* or Gustav-Adolf-Church in the Gumpendorferstrasse (6th District) was built 1846–49 by Theophil Hansen and Ludwig Förster as a 'Chapel of Toleration'.

123 The *Synagogue* in the Seitenstettengasse was built 1825–26 by Joseph Kornhäusel.

124 The fountain on the west side of the *Opera House*, like its counterpart on the other side – both were designed by van der Nüll and Siccardsburg – is decorated with statues by Hans Gasser.

125 The *Burgtheater*, formerly the Imperial Palace Theatre, was built 1874–88 by Carl Hasenauer to a design by Gottfried Semper to replace the old Court Theatre near the Palace on the Michaelerplatz. The restoration work following bomb-damage in 1945 was carried out by Michael Engelhart, who redesigned the auditorium.

126 The *Loggia of the Opera House* with the scenes from 'The Magic Flute' painted by Moritz von Schwind in 1866–68 was virtually undamaged in the 1945 air-raids.

127 The charming Biedermeier house of 1803 in the Schreyvogelgasse on the way up to the Mölkerbastei has been erroneously associated with Schubert's *Dreimäderlhaus*.

128 Carriage and pair in the *Michaelerplatz*; in the background the Church of St Michael, its doorway surmounted by statues by Matielli.

118

119

120

118 AUSTRIA-BRUNNEN
119 UNIVERSITÄT
120 ALBERTINA

121 OPER
122 EVANGELISCHE
     KIRCHE AB
123 SYNAGOGE

121

122

123

124, 12
OPER

125
BURG-
THEA'

124

125

126

129   The *Post Office Savings Bank* building of 1904–06 is one of Otto Wagner's main works. The façade is covered with granite slabs studded with aluminium nails and is surmounted by two aluminium statues by Otmar Schinkowitz. The bust of Georg Koch (1842–90), founder of the Post Office Savings Bank, is by Hans Scherpe and has stood in the Georg-Koch Platz in front of the building since 1913.

130   The *Karlsplatz* with the *Station* built by Otto Wagner for the Municipal Railway between 1893 and 1902; behind, Hansen's *Musikverein* building of 1867–69.

131–132   The '*Secession*' building was designed by Joseph Olbrich in 1897–98 as an exhibition hall for works of the Viennese 'Art Nouveau'. The dome is covered with gilded iron bay-leaves. The metal doors were designed by Gustav Klimt. The bronze statue of the triumvir Mark Anthony at the north-east corner was designed by Artur Strasser in 1899–1900.

133   The *Church am Steinhof*, dedicated to St Leopold, is situated on the Baumgartner Höhe, the site of a large hospital for mental and nervous diseases. The church was built by Otto Wagner in 1904–07. (See also the sketch-plan on p. 115.)

134   The *Villa* which *Otto Wagner* built for himself in 1913 in the Hüttelbergstrasse (14th District), makes an interesting comparison with the first villa he built in 1888, which is situated near by and which, in keeping with the period, is more elaborate.

135   The *Crematorium* in the gardens of the former 'Neugebäude', built by the Emperor Maximilian II in 1569 and surrounded by a fortified wall, was designed by Clemens Holzmeister in 1923 and represents the expressionism of the 'twenties.

136   Altred Roller, the great scenic artist and one of the leading members of the Viennese 'Secession', was responsible for the mosaics over the entrance to the Neo-Gothic *Breitensee Church*, built 1895–98 in the 14th District.

137   The building known as the *Loos-Haus* on the Michaeler-Platz was built by Adolf Loos in 1910 and became the prototype of a 'functional' style of architecture which dispensed with ornamentation.

138   The *Stadthalle* on the Vogelweidplatz (15th District) with its sports arenas was built by Roland Rainer for the Vienna Municipality.

139   The *Schottenpassage* (1961) with its escalators and its underground station, is one of several subways on the Ring, which were built to ease the growing traffic problems of the city.

140 The *Karl-Marx-Hof* in the Heiligenstädter Strasse (19th District), a tenement block with some 1,300 flats, was built 1927–30 by Karl Ehn and was the show-piece of the communal building programme which the Social Democrat administration carried through so energetically in the period between the wars.

141 Air view (Photo the Municipal Press Office) of the *Housing Estate in the Altmannsdorff Strasse*: Its tenement blocks are typical products of the building boom which has transformed the outer suburbs since the 1950s.

142 The *Karl Renner Memorial* near the Parliament building was unveiled in 1967 to commemorate the Social Democrat statesman who took over the Austrian Chancellorship after the collapse of 1918 and who, as Chancellor, Foreign Minister and President of the National Council, played a leading part in the rehabilitation of the Austrian Republic. Design by Josef Krawina, sculpture by Alfred Hrdlitschka.

143 The *Ringturm* on the corner of the Schottenring and Franz-Joseph Quay was built by Erich Boltenstern in 1953–55.

144 The Zacherl House on the corner of Brandstätte and Wildpretmarkt, built 1903–05 by Josef Plecnik, was one of the first modern, multi-storey buildings in the city centre.

145 The entrance to the *Wienfluss Tunnel*, like the western entrance to the Municipal Park, was built in 1906 by Friedrich Ohmann in the Secession style. Behind it is the Hotel Interkontinental, built in 1964. (Architects: Karl Appel and Walter Jaksch.)

146 The *Reichsbrücke* over the Danube, originally called the Kronprinz-Rudolf-Brücke, was built 1872–76 to link Leopoldstadt with the Kaisermühlen residential area, which came into being as a result of the Danube Conservancy scheme of 1871–75. In 1934 the bridge was repaired and after 1945 was rebuilt; from then until 1956 it was known as the Red Army Bridge.

147 The *Philips Building*, which stands on a rise overlooking the southern approach-road into Vienna (Triesterstrasse), was built 1961–63 by Prof. Dr Karl Schwanger and first occupied in February 1965.

148 This building on the Dr Karl-Lueger-Ring, designed by Prof. Karl Appel, dates from 1965–67.

149 The elegant reception building at *Schwechat Airport* was built by Pfeffer, Klandy, Hoch and Schimka in 1960.

150–151 Biedermeier inns on the Cobenzlgasse in *Grinzing*, where the Heurige or new wine, product of the surrounding vineyards, is served.

152 The *Vineyards of Nussdorf* on the Nussberg. (See also colour plate X, page 99.)

153 The Beethoven House on the Pfarrplatz in *Heiligenstadt*. (See also illustrations 92–94.)

154 The eighty-year-old Richard Strauss conducts the Vienna Philharmonic in the great *Hall of the Musikverein*. (Photo Lothar Rübelt.)

13

135
KREMA-
TORIUM

WIE DER HIRSCH NACH DER QUELLE SO SCHREIET
MEINE SEELE GOTT NACH DIR   PSM 41.

136
ITENSEER-
KIRCHE

145

146

147

148

RICHARD
STRAUSS

Chronology

Sources

Index

976 Emperor Otto II confers the County of Austria (Ostmark) on a Franconian family, the Babenbergs.

c. 1135 The Babenbergs gain possession of Vienna, which is referred to, for the first time, as 'civitas' in 1137.

1147 Eastern part of the parish church of St Stephen consecrated.

1156 Emperor Frederick I Barbarossa elevates Austria to the rank of Duchy.

Duke Heinrich II 'Jasomirgott' (1156–77) moves his residence from Leopoldsberg near Klosterneuburg to Vienna.

1221 Duke Leopold VI the Glorious (1194–1230) confers on Vienna its first traditional civic right, which allows the citizens to trade with Hungary and to hold a market.

1246 Duke Friedrich II, last of the Babenbergs, dies.

1246–76 Period of the so-called Interregnum, during which, from 1251, King Premysl Ottokar II of Bohemia rules over Vienna.

1263 Extension to St Stephen's consecrated.

1278 Following a decisive battle against Ottokar on the Marchfeld, King Rudolf of Habsburg enters Vienna.

1281 Rudolf I appoints his son Albrecht I Regent and gains the approval of the Reichstag in Augsburg for the investiture of his sons Albrecht and Rudolf II as Dukes with the Babenberg estates.

1296 Albrecht confers new civic rights on Vienna (Albertinum I).

1298 Albrecht I becomes King of Germany.

1340 Consecration of the Gothic choir of St Stephen's.

1349 One of the great plagues that afflict Vienna periodically is rampant.

1365 Duke Rudolf IV (1358–65) founds the University and elevates St Stephen's to the diocesan foundation of the Duchy.

1438 Duke Albrecht V, who has ruled since 1404, is elected German Emperor as Albrecht II; from then until 1740 the imperial title remains with the Habsburgs, who reside for most of that time in Vienna.

1408 Burgomaster Konrad Vorlauf, involved in a dispute between Dukes Leopold and Ernst, is executed.

1421 Inquisition condemns 210 Jews to be burnt publicly at the stake.

1453 Emperor Friedrich III (Duke of Austria 1424–93 as Friedrich V) makes Austria an Archduchy.

1462 Emperor Friedrich in a dispute with his brother Albrecht VI is besieged in Vienna Castle.

1463 Burgomaster Wolfgang Holzer is executed.

1469 (1479) Vienna becomes a Bishopric and St Stephen's a Cathedral.

1485–90 Vienna is occupied by King Matthias Corvinus of Hungary.
Maximilian I (Emperor 1493–1519) drives the Hungarians out of Vienna.

1517 Maximilian I issues new civic laws which give the ruler greater influence over the election of Burgomaster and Council.

1521 Karl V (Emperor since 1519) transfers the German possessions of the Habsburgs to his brother Ferdinand I, who becomes Roman King in 1531 and finally Emperor in 1556 following the abdication of Karl V.

1522 Burgomaster Dr Martin Siebenbürger and five members of the City Council are executed.

1526 New municipal and police regulations abolish the privileges of the citizens and concentrate power in the hands of the Land authorities.

1528 An Edict by Ferdinand I forbids Jews to ply a trade or own property.

1529 From 19 September until 14 October Vienna is besieged by the Turkish Sultan Suleiman II and successfully defended by Count Niklas Salm.

1551 The Jesuits are summoned to Vienna to contend with the marked spread of Protestantism.

1564–76 Emperor Maximilian II.

1576–1612 Emperor Rudolf II, who resides mainly in Prague, supports the Counter-Reformation; in 1577 the Protestants are forbidden to practise their religion in public.

c. 1598 Construction of the Danube Canal.

1612–19 Emperor Matthias.

1619–37 Emperor Ferdinand II, nephew of his predecessor and first of the Styrian line of the Habsburgs to come to the throne.

1624 The Jews are expelled from the city to a ghetto in Leopoldstadt.

1637–57 Emperor Ferdinand III.

1643 and 1645 The Swedish army threatens Vienna.

1652 The 'Reformation Patent' ensures the final victory of the Counter-Reformation.

1657–1705 Emperor Leopold I.

1679 The Plague claims many victims. Abraham a Sancta Clara in his sermons calls on the Viennese to repent.

1683 From 14 July to 12 September Vienna is besieged a second time by the Turks, this time under the Grand Vizier Kara Mustapha; the defence is conducted by Count Rüdiger von Starhemberg. The relieving army under Duke Charles of Lorraine and King Jan Sobieski of Poland defeats the Turks in the battle on the Kahlenberg.

1693 Prince Eugene of Savoy, who has been in the Imperial service since 1683, becomes Field-marshal and Commander-in-Chief against the Turks.

1698 Czar Peter the Great visits Vienna. The Emperor confers new privileges on the city, enabling it to acquire land in the suburbs.

1703 The first clearing-bank is established, followed on 24 December 1705 by a special charter setting up the Vienna Municipal Bank.

1704 The Line Walls are built round the suburbs, mainly to protect them against Hungarian marauders.

1705–11 Emperor Joseph I.

1705 The Academy of Fine Arts is opened.

1711–40 Emperor Karl VI, last of the male line of Habsburgs. The Pragmatic Sanction of 1713 ensures succession to the Habsburg domains by his eldest daughter Maria Theresa (the imperial throne passes in 1742 to the Wittelsbachs when Karl Albert, King of Bohemia, becomes Karl VII).

1713–14 Vienna's last great plague.

1718 Porcelain factory established in Rossau. About the same period other industries start up in the suburbs and are protected by customs duties.

1722 Vienna becomes an Archbishopric.

1729 Pietro Metastasio succeeds Apostolo Zeno as 'poeta cesareo' (Poet Laureate).

1740–80 Maria Theresa reigns as Archduchess of Austria, Queen of Bohemia and Queen of Hungary. In 1736 she had married Duke Franz Stefan of Lorraine-Tuscany, whom she appoints co-Regent and who is elected German Emperor in 1745. After his death in 1765 Maria Theresa appoints her son Joseph II co-Regent.

1742 The Freemasons' Lodge 'Zu den drei Kammern' is founded.

1746 The Jesuits found the Theresianische Kollegium in the Favorita Castle.

1749 Gerard van Swieten, summoned to Vienna in 1745 by Maria Theresa, produces his plan for the reform of medical studies and subsequently founds the First Viennese Medical School.

1751 Maria Theresa introduces censorship of the theatre.

1754 At the instigation of Prince Kaunitz the Oriental Academy for the Study of Oriental Languages is founded; Academy of Engineering established.

Gluck is appointed Court Kapellmeister.

1761 The German Society for the Cultivation of German Language and Literature is founded.

1762 Klemm and Herrl produce Vienna's first weekly periodical *Die Welt*.

First performance of Gluck's 'Orfeo ed Euridice'.

1764 A law of 5 May gives the Jews the right to form a community of their own.

1766 Joseph II opens the Prater, until then an imperial hunting-preserve, to the public.

1771 Maria Theresa's Stock Exchange Charter.

1773 The Order of Jesuits is disbanded.

1774 A plan of educational reform by Abbot Johann Ignaz von Felbiger is introduced for the German schools.

1775 Joseph II throws the Augarten open to the public.

1780 The periodical *Diarium*, founded at the begininng of the century, appears as the *Wiener Zeitung*.

1780–90 Joseph II becomes sole ruler following his previous election as German Emperor in 1765.

1781 As part of the reforms instituted by Joseph II, censorship of the theatre is lifted (11 June) and the Edict of Toleration is issued (13–17 October). The Emperor charges the government to introduce a system of poor relief.

1782 Dissolution of the monasteries. Pope Pius VI visits Vienna. First performances of Mozart's 'Il Seraglio'.

1783 Reform of the administration.

1784 Joseph II founds the General Hospital.

1785 Foundation of the Academy of Surgical Medicine for the training of army doctors.

1786 First performance of Mozart's 'The Marriage of Figaro'.

1790–92 Emperor Leopold II, previously Duke of Tuscany, succeeds his childless brother.

1791 First performance of 'The Magic Flute'.

1792–1835 Emperor Franz II (Franz I of Austria from 1804) succeeds his father. Joseph II's reforms are rescinded.

1797 First performance of Haydn's 'The Creation'.

1804　The Archduchy of Austria is declared an Empire (11 August).

1805　Murat enters Vienna (13 November) and Napoleon sets up his headquarters for a few days at Schönbrunn.

First performance of Beethoven's 'Fidelio'.

1806　On 6 August Franz II renounces the title of German Emperor and the Holy Roman Empire comes to an end.

1807　Josef Schreyvogel founds the *Sonntagsblatt*. Vinzenz von Kern founds the Institute of Surgery.

1809　Second occupation of Vienna by the French and on 15 August Napoleon's birthday is celebrated with great pomp.

1811　The National Exchequer is faced with bankruptcy.

1814　From 1 January the semi-official *Wiener Zeitung* appears daily. From 2 November 1814 until 11 June 1815 the Congress of Vienna meets, presided over by Prince Metternich.

1815　The Vienna Polytechnic is founded.

1816　On 1 July the National Bank is opened.

1824　First performance of Beethoven's Ninth Symphony.

1835–48　Reign of Emperor Ferdinand I (d. 1875).

1835　Ferdinand's Water Conduit System. First trade exhibition.

1837　Ludwig Wilhelm R. von Mauthner founds a Children's Hospital. On 23 November the first Viennese railway, the Emperor Ferdinand Northern Line, is opened in Floridsdorf.

1845　Gas lighting is introduced.

1847　The Academy of Sciences is founded.

246

1848　On 13 March the Estates of Lower Austria meet in the 'Ständehaus' on the Herrengasse. Street demonstrations lead to riots; there are 44 dead. State Chancellor Metternich bows to the popular demand for his resignation.

On 15 March the Emperor Ferdinand is greeted with jubilation as he drives through the city. He issues a manifesto approving a new Constitution.

On 25 April the new constitution is announced.

On 15 May fresh demonstrations by workers and students demanding: 'Only one Chamber! Union with Germany!'

On 25 May the 'Academic Legion' is dissolved; barricades are erected and the dissolution decree is withdrawn. National Guards and students set up a Security Committee.

On 27 May the government places the city under the protection of the Security Committee.

On 3 July the newspaper *Die Presse*, founded by August Zwang, appears, its first editor-in-chief Dr Leopold Landsteiner.

On 22 July the Reichstag, elected by universal suffrage, meets in the Riding School.

On 12 August the court, which had retired to Innsbrook, returns to Vienna.

On 6 October, during a march-past, General Count Breda is shot by a grenadier. In the rioting that follows War Minister Latour is lynched and his body hung on a lamp-post. A rioting mob streams in from the suburbs.

On 7 October the Arsenal is evacuated by the Polish garrison and plundered by the mob. The court moves to Olmütz.

On 13 October troops, mostly Croats, move in on the city. The shops are closed; the Communal Council mobilizes all men fit for military service.

On 15 October Citizens' Free Corps are organized under Messenhauser's command.

On 22 October Field Marshal Windischgrätz declares a state of siege and Vienna is completely surrounded.

On 28 October, after negotiations with Windisch-grätz have broken down, Croatian troops storm the barricades on the Praterstern and push forward into the suburbs.

On 31 October the centre of the city is also occupied by Windischgrätz, who sets up a military régime; on 9 November Robert Blum, visiting delegate from the Frankfurt Parliament, is executed, on 16 November Messenhauser, the defender, is shot, and on 23 November the editors of the 'Radikal', Dr Becker and Dr Jellinek, also face a firing-squad.

On 20 November Prince Schwarzenburg forms a government, and on 2 December Ferdinand I abdicates in favour of his nephew Franz Joseph I.

1849 The 34 suburban districts are brought within the jurisdiction of the Municipality of Vienna.

1850 The 'First Municipal Expansion' is put into effect, when the suburbs are incorporated with the city proper in one municipality and eight Districts are formed.

1855 The conclusion of the Concordat on 18 August marks a new high-water mark in the reactionary tide, which finds expression, for example, in a further tightening of the censorship.

1857 The Emperor orders the demolition of the fortifications and a competition is announced for the design of the new Ring.

1860 A parliamentary system is introduced in October with an Upper and a Lower House. Jews are given permission to own real property.

1861 In February a new and more liberal local government constitution is introduced.

1862 Jews are given active and passive voting rights. Rokitansky opens the Institute of Pathological Anatomy.

1864 The *Neue Freie Presse* is founded, edited by Max Friedländer, Michael Etienna and Adolf Werthner.

1865 The Ring is opened. On 4 October the first horse-drawn tram starts from the Schottentor.

1867 The Associations' Law of 14 November lays the foundations of political parties. The surgeon Theodor Billroth moves from Zurich to Vienna. The *Neue Wiener Tagblatt* is founded.

1868 Confessional legislation guarantees freedom of worship to non-Catholics.

1868–78 Golden era of the liberal City Government under Cajetan Felder.

Regulation of the Danube.

1873 The brilliant opening of the World Exhibition in May is followed by a severe stock-exchange crisis. Vienna's first Water Conduit System is completed.

1874 The Central Cemetery is opened.

First performance of 'Die Fledermaus' by Johann Strauss.

1881 The Ring Theatre is burnt down on 8 December: 386 die.

1888 The Christian Social Party is founded.

1892 The 'Second Municipal Expansion' on 1 January incorporates a further 33 suburbs.

1895–1902 The Municipal Railway is built.

1897 Theodor Herzl founds the Zionist weekly *Die Welt*.

1897–1910 Municipal politics dominated by the anti-Semitic, Christian Social Burgomaster Karl Lueger.

1900 In the local government elections of 31 May the first two Social Democrats are elected.

1901 Martin Buber takes over the editorship of *Die Welt*.

1904 The 'Second Municipal Expansion' finally incorporates districts on the left bank of the Danube.

1905 First performance of Lehár's 'The Merry Widow'.

1916 Following the death of Franz Joseph on 21 November at Schönbrunn, he is succeeded by the Emperor Karl I for the remaining two years of the Habsburg monarchy.

1918 Following the armistice of 11 November, Karl I abdicates and on 12 November the German–Austrian Republic is proclaimed.

1919 The Peace Treaty between Austria and the Allied Powers is signed at St Germain. In the first general and secret elections for the Municipal Council the Social Democrats gain 100 out of 165 seats.

1921 Vienna becomes a Land in the Federal Republic.

1923–24 Karl Seitz, one of the Social Democrat co-founders of the Republic, becomes Burgomaster.

1927 During violent workers' demonstrations the Palace of Justice is set on fire.

1934 The predominantly Christian Social government of the Republic appoints a government commissar to govern Vienna. On 25 July Federal Chancellor Dollfuss is murdered by a National Socialist. Demonstrations by the German-supported Nazis increase in violence.

1938 The Schuschnigg Government yields to internal and external pressure, and on 14 March Hitler makes his triumphal entry into Vienna, which ceases to be the capital of an independent State.

1945 On 7 to 13 April Soviet troops occupy the city, damaged by bombing. On 27 April the Second Austrian Republic is proclaimed. The Social Democrat General Theodor Körner, who is to become Federal President in 1951, is elected Burgomaster of Vienna.

1951–65 Franz Jonas is Burgomaster, becoming Federal President in 1965

1955 On 15 May in the Upper Belvedere the Austrian State Treaty is signed, bringing the Allied occupation to an end.

Sources of Quotations and Illustrations

Quotations

BAHR, HERMANN: *Erinnerungen an Burkhard* (Berlin 1913), *Expressionismus* (Munich 1919) 103, 114

BAUERNFELD, EDUARD VON: *Aus Alt- und Neuwien* (Vienna 1881) 82

BERLIOZ, HECTOR: *Mémoires* (Paris 1848) 101

BURNEY: *Dr Burney's Musical Tour in Europe*, Vol. II. edited by A. Scholles (London 1959) 38, 67

CELEBI, EVLIYA: *Im Reiche des goldenen Apfels* (1665), edited by R. K. Kreutel (Verlag Styria, Graz 1957) 56

Encyclopédie, edited by DIDEROT AND D'ALEMBERT, Vol. VIII (Neufchastel 1765) 38, 41

ENGELS, FRIEDRICH: *Marx/Engels*, complete edition, Section I, Vol. 6 (Marx-Engels-Verlag, Berlin 1932) 92

GRILLPARZER, FRANZ: *Dem Andenken Schreyvogels* (1832), *Erinnerungen aus dem Jahre 1848, Gedichte* 55, 82

HILLER, FERDINAND: *Aus dem Tonleben unserer Zeit*, New Series (1867) 72

HOFMANNSTHAL, HUGO VON: *Reden und Aufsätze*, Vol. III of the collected works (S. Fischer, Berlin 1924) 31

LOTHAR, RUDOLF: *Das Wiener Burgtheater* (Leipzig 1899) 75

MONTAGUE, LADY MARY WORTLEY: *Letters* (London 1861) 41, 84

MONTESQUIEU, CHARLES DE: *Voyages de Montesquieu* (Bordeaux 1894–96) 55

MOZART, LEOPOLD AND WOLFGANG AMADEUS: *Die Briefe W.A. Mozarts und seiner Familie, Kritische Gesamtausgabe von Ludwig Schiedermeier* (Georg Müller, Munich 1914) 67

REICHARDT, JOHANN FRIEDRICH: *Vertraute Briefe, geschrieben auf einer Reise nach Wien und den österreichischen Staaten* (1810) 56

SCHUMANN, ROBERT: *Neue Zeitschrift für Musik* of 10 March 1840 73

SEITZ, KARL, quoted from the *Wien-Chronik* edited by Jost Perfahl (Salzburg 1961) 113

WAGNER, RICHARD: *Briefe an Minna Wagner*, Vol. 1 (Berlin 1908) 93

Illustrations

The author thanks the following for providing photographs to supplement his own: Landesbildstelle Wien-Burgenland, No. 39, 60; Mr H. Kopezki, Vienna, No. 30, 32; Pressestelle der Stadt Wien, No. 141; Mr Lothar Rübelt, Vienna, No. 77, 151. The drawings are based on originals in the Archive of Atlantis Verlag, the Central Library, and the collection of prints and drawings of the ETH, in Zurich.

Index

The numbers printed in italic refer to the black-and-white photographs